About the Aut

MW00568824

I believe he and Barbara Cartland are the
two finest writers in the world today.
*Chris Tarrant, Capital Radio,
on Jack De Ladd's previous works*

Your Place or Mine?

The Complete Chat-Up Book

Jack De Ladd

CENTURY
London Sydney Auckland Johannesburg

Copyright © Jack De Ladd 1989

All rights reserved

First published in 1989 by Century
Hutchinson Ltd, Brookmount House,
62–65 Chandos Place, Covent Garden,
London WC2N 4NW

Century Hutchinson Australia Pty Ltd,
89–91 Albion Street, Surry Hills,
New South Wales 2010, Australia

Century Hutchinson New Zealand
Limited, PO Box 40–086, Glenfield,
Auckland 10, New Zealand

Century Hutchinson South Africa
(Pty) Ltd, PO Box 337, Bergvlei,
2012 South Africa

Designed by Martin Lovelock

Cover cartoons by Bill Belcher

Photoset in Linotron Baskerville by
Deltatype Ltd, Ellesmere Port, Cheshire

Printed and bound in Great Britain by
Anchor Press Ltd, Tiptree, Essex

British Library Cataloguing in Publication
Data

De Ladd, Jack, *1951–*
    Your place or mine? the complete chat-up book
    1. Sex relations. Seduction – Humour
    I. Title
    306.7′34′0207

ISBN 0 7126 1837 6

Contents

Acknowledgements

First of all, a profound thanks to the battery of celebrities who were talkative enough to help with this 'fun' project. Those who I successfully chatted up in this direction included: Dave Barrett, Tony Blackburn, Paul Coia, Norman Collier, Steve Colman, Leslie Crowther, Bobby Davro, John Francombe, Michael Groth, Frazer Hines, Liz Hobbs, Phil Holden, Jools Holland, Sally Jones, John Kettley, Eddie Large, Don Maclean, Richard O'Sullivan, Su Pollard, Sue Robbie, Alan Robson, Chris Tarrant, Gillian Taylforth, Clive Warren, Lizzie Webb, Simon Williams and Wincey Willis.

The idea was Anthony Cheetham's and I must thank him sincerely, plus others at Century Hutchinson who successfully guided me through the project, notably Sarah Wallace and Heather Holden-Brown.

More pertinently, this work involved phenomenal research: I would like to express public gratitude to the publishers of all Britain's national newspapers, rock and pop magazines, plus *Time* and *Newsweek* for providing the raw material. There is also the matter of some 200 books; as with particular newspaper editions, these are listed alongside the particular gems culled. A special mention to Irving Wallace for *The Intimate Sex Lives of Famous People* (1982), John Atkins for *Sex in Literature* (1970), E.S. Turner for *A History of Courting* (1977), and J.J. Gabay for *The Little Black Book* (1985). Otherwise, if anyone feels unjustly omitted they are invited to 'chat up' myself (or in the men's case, Sarah Wallace) for inclusion of a source line in future editions.

A First Line of Chat

They are the most important words you will ever speak. Chosen rightly, they can – and do – bring romance, joy, fulfilment (yes, even sex); they can forge relationships lasting 60 years or more. Chosen wrongly, your chance has almost certainly gone for ever.

This book celebrates that great romantic institution, the chat-up line, and distils the great one-liners of the leaders in the art. Read it for fun, or use it as the ultimate self-help guide to turn feverish moments of first meeting into triumph!

The tuition in how-to-win-the-boy-or- girl-of-your-dreams-in-eleven-well-chosen-words comes at a time when never has a good 'ice-breaker' been needed more. The Aids-inspired climate of caution tends to make any first time introducee these days eye one coldly and suspiciously over the rim of their vodka and tonic. But perhaps no more!

Much of the secret of flirting successfully with the opposite sex is, of course, lateral thinking, ('how would you like to do some thinking laterally?' being a chat-up line in itself). Therefore a vast store of knowledge gleaned from many parts of the globe follows, with the required minimum only, I hope, of such hoary old chestnuts as: 'Do you come here often?'; 'Are you on holiday or do you live here?'; 'Is this a private orgy or can anyone join in?'; 'I veel say thees and I veel say eet urnhly ehwunce,' not to mention Samantha Fox's personal *mot noir* – 'I didn't recognise you with your clothes on'.

Certainly if romantic introduction is an art form in itself, it is sad to report that we no longer see so many lights from yonder window breaking while young men exclaim 'Oh speak, my bright angel, for thou art glorious . . .' (Romeo to Juliet); 'By the fire that quickens

Nilus slime, I go from hence, thy soldier, servant . . .' (Antony to Cleopatra); not to mention 'Would that I had thy inches' (Cleopatra to Antony).

But with chapters following giving the golden lovelines of Hollywood plus the best of history's love letters and poems, it is to be hoped some charm and grace may be encouraged to return to the once noble art of courtship. You know the sort of thing: 'If you don't submit willingly, by God I'll take you as the trappers in the old days used to take the squaws' (*The Land of Promise* by Somerset Maugham). Joking aside, it is undoubtedly subtlety that is the key to successful seduction. Low lights, mood music and a soft voice have long been seen as key elements in making one's chosen quarry passive enough for passion.

Extensive research for this book (2012 nights spent in an array of European discotheques, a year and a half hiding under a table in the ballroom of the QE2, and two weeks at the annual sociologists' conference at Sussex University) has, however, shown the definitive answer to the age-old riddle of how to approach the opposite sex. Basically the first, decisive chat-up line should impose a debt. The trick is to make one's intended victim so keen to prove something they will spend hours and hours talking to you to do just that. This is well-illustrated by the case of Edward VIII and Mrs Simpson (see p. 12). It also explains why macho medallion-clad males with that disco swagger always say that the secret of their success is 'you just insult 'em, don'tcha'.

Thus three perfect lines upon meeting a member of the opposite sex to whom a woman took a fancy would be: 'I bet you can't spell Zbigniew Brzezinski,'; 'You don't look to me as if you could swim five yards without sinking,'; and 'Everyone knows all men with moustaches are wimps.' They will scarcely be away from your side as they determinedly try to prove they are (a) intelligent; (b) athletic; or (c) a he-man.

An injection of wit works wonders, too, of course. In profoundly thanking the numerous celebrities who sent me their own favourite and bugbear lines, I am still chortling at Su Pollard's being approached in an up-market cocktail bar and being asked: 'What's a naff girl like you doing in a place like this?' I am also still smirking at Bobby Davro's comic interrogative: 'Do you know the difference between the male sexual organ and a leg of chicken?' Answer – 'No.' 'OK then, let's go on a picnic.'

In compiling this exhaustive (you can say that again) work, I have naturally been asked again and again for the definitive chat-up manoeuvre, the one that really works. All I can say is that I have discovered the worst self-introduction of all time. It runs: 'You won't believe me, but I am compiling the definitive book on chatting up the opposite sex and . . .' This all-time non-starter is inevitably followed by a kick on the shin or a glass of wine over the cerebal regions, and that is if one is on the fortunate side.

Naturally I have my favourites. I do not know whether to fall prostrate in admiration or laughter at Terence Trent D'Arby: 'Darling you have to tell me your real name, because last night in my dreams I could only call you baby.' I certainly admire the approach of the late *Who* drummer Keith Moon, who used to bribe waiters to have the companions of likely lasses ejected from leading night clubs.

But certainly I gasp in awe at the approach of love-hungry youth in the Soviet bloc, as told by E. S. Turner (*The History of Courting*). He quotes these romantic blockbusters: 'The night inspires me to over-fulfil my quota by a higher and higher percentage. I fell in love with your working achievement from the very first moment.' Not to mention 'I am singing a song of my motor and all the leather straps sing with me because tonight I am going to kiss my sweetheart and I am going to repeat to her that plant number three holds the record.'

Perhaps the most enigmatic reply I received from the ranks of the famous came from Frazer Hines of Emmerdale Farm renown, whom I had asked for his favourite recipe for attracting the opposite sex. He sent me back instructions on how to make an omelette – 'that's the only recipe I know'.

Like many a young man with something of an attraction for the opposite sex, he couldn't be serious . . . or could he? I suggest you read on.

Jack De Ladd

1

Making the Most of First Encounters of the Close Kind

There are certain crucial preparations any budding Valentino or Grace Jones must make before attempting to devastate the opposite sex. After consulting a number of leading Lotharios, three witch doctors, two professors of sexology from Bangkok and the author's great-aunt Mabel, we give you eight golden rules to ensure you come out on top:

1 Plan ahead Treat the whole process as you would a military engagement; or, if like Prince Edward you don't see yourself as a Royal Marine, a game of snooker. In other words: prepare, assess risk, aim—and fire! (Assessing the risk means making sure there's no boyfriend/girlfriend lurking around at the time . . . as Noel Coward said, no brief encounter is worth two black eyes and a broken jaw.)

2 Speak softly (we won't complete the quotation with 'and carry a big stick'). (This is a non-sexist publication.) Space precludes a long psychological explanation of why, but talking in hushed tones will increase your attractiveness to the opposite sex. Shsh! Honest!

3 Flatter and cajole as if your life depended on it. If you don't know what cajole means, flatter twice as much instead.

4 Smile as if you're a walking ad for Pepsodent.

5 Use touch (just as any good rugby player would). Or rather, the hint of touch. But not like you are practising semaphore signals. Don't grope. Offer to wash their hair or paint their toenails (especially the men).

6 Clean your fingernails (or paint them).

7 Wash your hair at least once a month.

8 Remember, practice makes perfect.

Think of yourself as Laurence Olivier or Ronald Reagan. Rehearse your lines carefully—in front of a mirror if you like. Hum romantic tunes to yourself culled from the hairspray advertisements. And *don't* put on a different voice, a wig or a toupee. Even *Dynasty* fans can sometimes spot a phoney.

You memorized that? Now read on.

2

Just to Prove There's Nothing New Under the Sun

Oldies but Goldies?

So you think his/her chat-up line is tired and jaded? Well, some of the oldies have been known to work:

'Would you like to dance?' Yes, unbelievably these were the first words spoken by blond connoisseur and collector **Rod Stewart** to one girl who was to become his live-in girlfriend, **Dee Harrington**. She told how he came into a Hollywood party 'wearing a white velvet suit and looking like an Omo advert'.

'I watched him as he disentangled himself from one girl after another . . . but still they kept throwing themselves at him. After a while, I suddenly became aware that he was staring at me . . .' Miss Harrington came to realize 'with a state of shock' that he was actually *shy*. 'About half an hour before the club was due to close, he tapped my foot with his to get my attention and said nervously, "Would you like to dance?" '

From the *Sunday Mirror*, 8 February 1978

Top Spots for Hot Shots

BEST ON-GOING SITUATIONS FOR GIRLS TO MEET MEN

Sharing a taxi ('just keep driving round the block')

At a snooker club (but wait for your cue)

By the tavern at a cricket match (the rest are too busy watching the game)

Car mechanics classes

Hang gliding (but keep your feet on the ground)

In an airport lounge (just think of all those high-flying executives all waiting for hours for the fog to clear)

At the Young Conservatives annual conference (ratio 20:1, according to the *Daily Telegraph*)

In a hotel coffee shop

Wind surfing
Out jogging   } If you don't mind the cold
At a soccer match

At the newsagents on Sunday mornings

At a garage (if you can stand the oil and grease)

Trawling the riverbank during an angling contest

At a running club

At a political demo

Polo (but only if you're looking for a rich husband)

On a singles holiday

In a pub near a barracks

The buffet bar on an Inter-City train

At the local soccer club (sadly most of them only have eyes for the ball)

At a court of law (you could meet a rich barrister—but just as easily a villain. Tip: the latter look the more affluent)

T A Kung Fu lesson

'Would you like to go into films?' This excruciating chestnut amazingly helped **Roger Vadim** hook one of the twentieth century's greatest beauties—**Brigitte Bardot**. His question came in a letter, 'If you would and it would interest you to make a test, telephone me' on behalf of producer Marc Allegret. She came for the test. Her eyes met Vadim's. She drew attention to herself by walking out on to a balcony . . . and you might say, Pow! The thunderbolt struck.

This really is upsetting, we know, but a similar line was used by producer **Carlo Ponti** on the beautiful **Sophia Loren**, whom he would eventually marry: 'Listen, I've launched many actresses like Alida Valli, Gina Lollobrigida; it was for me that they made their first appearances in films; I can do the same for you . . .' And yes, 'Come to my office tomorrow, I'd like you to make a test for a film.' She agonized, but happily a straightforward business relationship preceded romance.

Today's equivalent is of course, 'How would you like to be in my next video?' and, according to singer **Shirley Holliman** in the *Sun*, was a mainstay for Wham! stars **George Michael** and **Andrew Ridgeley**. 'It is one of the best chat-up lines in the world,' she said. 'It works every time.'

From the Sunday Express magazine, *9 September 1984; Donald Zec, 'Sophia: An Intimate Biography', 1975; the* Sun, *16 October 1984*

'Just for an hour or so. It'll be good for you.' Another success, this time from later President **Gerald Ford** when he asked young divorcée **Betty Warren** for a date. She refused at first, saying 'as a lawyer you ought to understand that,' but finally agreed on the short option, which was to lead them to the altar.

From Gerald R. Ford, 'A Time to Heal', 1979

'Let's go upstairs, m'dear, and do funny things with our bodies.' This delicious line certainly worked, according to **Malcolm Muggeridge**, who reported its use by the short, stout, squeaky-voiced **H. G. Wells** on a young and beautiful lady at a party. 'And was it funny?' asked Muggeridge to the lady in later life. 'Not very,' she replied.

From the Daily Mirror, *22 May 1984*

'**Has anybody told you you're a very pretty girl?**' I know you can't believe me, but according to **Elizabeth Taylor** in her book, *Elizabeth Taylor: An Informal Memoir*, this wretched old chestnut was the opening gambit of the great Welsh superstud **Richard Burton**. 'And I said to myself, "Oy, gevaldt, here's the great lover, the great wit, the great intellectual of Wales, and he comes out with a line like that". I couldn't believe it. I couldn't wait to go back to the dressing room where all the girls were and tell them.' Later Miss Taylor softened. She was tired and confused after a near brush with death in London, and seeing him incapacitated with 'trembling fits' from a hangover, his face covered in red blotches, he fluffed a line and 'my heart just went out to him.'

From John Cotterell and Fergus Cashin; 'Richard Burton: An Intimate Biography', *1971*

BEST ON-GOING SITUATIONS FOR MEN TO MEET GIRLS

Knitting or tapestry classes
Outside a school at 3.30 pm (only if you melt at the sight of rampaging runny-nosed kids)
Teacher training college
In the bar after a ballet
In a 'Body Shop' (no jokes that it's a body you're after, please)
Horse riding
At a hockey international (but only if you can scream)
On a Mediterranean cruise
In the womenswear department of a chain store
At a mixed aerobics class
Any puny stretch of grass on a summer's afternoon
Wine bars at lunchtime
Alcoholics Anonymous
Flea markets

Wrestling bouts
Delicatessens
A unisex hairdresser
Outside a ladies toilet (but be careful about the other men hanging around!)

Madame, you are now sitting on the largest penis in the world. This rather risqué follow-up to 'Would you like to sit on my knee?' is of course usually left unspoken. It may also not have its basis in fact. But for Greek shipping magnate **Aristotle Onassis** it was often said and demonstrably true. In what most of his sophisticated guests thought a quite vulgar little joke, Mr Onassis had the bar stools on his 322-ft mega-yacht, the *Christina*, covered with white whale foreskin. **Greta Garbo** was among those unfortunate enough to be on the receiving end of Mr Onassis's rather gross chat-up line after she sat down on several square metres of whaleskin.

From Peter Evans, 'Ari: The Life and Times of Aristotle Socrates Onassis', 1986

Of the World's Most Exceedingly Famous Couples and How They 'Got it Together'

'LET'S GO, DEN' (OR 'CAN I GIVE YOU A LIFT TO THE STATION?')

Margaret Thatcher met husband **Denis** in the fairly unusual setting of a Conservative Association meeting in Dartford, Kent, to choose a General Election candidate. She was twenty-three at the time and naturally was chosen ahead of several more experienced male applicants. One of her supporters was one Major Denis Thatcher, MBE, mentioned in dispatches, who ran a local paint company at Erith. But despite her success, a problem emerged: Margaret was working in Colchester at the time and needed to get to work the next morning. Fortunately Denis came to her aid and drove her into London and to Liverpool Street in time to catch her last train to Colchester.

'Luckily Denis came to my rescue,' she said. He asked her for a date; she refused for three weeks, saying she was 'busy' but eventually gave way in what she told Barbara Walters became 'a deep romance'. He said: 'She was beautiful, very kind and thoughtful. Who could not meet Margaret and be completely slain by her personality and intellectual brilliance?' But one question has never been answered about the fateful first meeting: did *he* say to *her* 'Would you like a lift into London?' Or did she, characteristically, come out with the decisive chat-up line? You know, something like: 'Let's go, Den.'

From Tricia Murray, 'Margaret Thatcher', 1978; the Sunday Express *magazine, 7 December 1986;* Daily Mail, *21 March 1987*

CATCH A RISING STAR
Paul and **Linda McCartney** first met at a press party for the launch of the Beatles *Sergeant Pepper* album. **Linda Eastman**, an American magazine assistant, was known for her persistence in getting to know rock stars and had obtained her invitation by trading a photograph of **Brian Jones** of the Rolling Stones. At the photo session (invitations like gold-dust) she kept pointing her camera at Paul. With more persistence she obtained his unlisted phone number but, despite a barrage of calls, never reached him. Later, again by 'chance', they met at London's Bag o' Nails club and, according to Paul: 'I was in my little booth and she was in her little booth, and we were giving each other the eye, you know.' A year later they decided to get married.

From Peter Brown and Steve Gains, 'The Love You Make: An Inside Story of The Beatles', 1983

ON UNION BUSINESS
Ronald and **Nancy Reagan** met because he was a Bolshie shop steward at the time. Well, an active union man anyway, as secretary of the Screen Actors Guild. His chat-up line to young MGM starlet Nancy Davis: 'Hi, I'm Ronnie Reagan. If you don't mind a short dinner date, I'd be happy to talk to you about your problems.' Nancy's

problem was that in the days of blacklists, her name kept turning up on the lists of communist front organizations. She had approached 'fixit Ron' on the orders of her producer, **Mervyn Le Roy**. He said: 'Don't get ahead of me. Bells didn't ring or skyrockets explode, although I think perhaps they did. It was just that I had buried the part of me where such things happened so deep, I couldn't hear them.'

From Ronald Reagan, 'Where's the Rest of Me?' 1965

ZIP CODE

Bob Geldof met **Paula Yates**, who had just finished her A levels and was working as a char-lady in London (with her own squeegee, she said proudly) when she turned up in a weird attire at his promoter's office in Dublin, looked at him and said 'Hi.' He said hi, too; he was Bob Geldof. She said she'd met him before. 'Oh yeah, I remember,' said Saint Bob, though he didn't. 'There's nowhere to sit,' said she. 'Come and sit on my knee,' said he, never

one to see the needy suffer. Travelling later with him by limousine to a concert, she leaned across and unzipped his trousers. ' "Stop it, will you," I said half-heartedly,' said Bob later in his autobiography. ' "Christ, this one's been around," I thought. Afterwards she told me she thought she'd better do it because she'd imagined that's what all rock stars expected.'

Later, he decided he didn't want a long-term relationship. She followed him to Paris and, when he came out of a gig, there she was standing in the snow in a ballgown. She went on to turn up at his home with her own sheets and a Harrods hamper. 'I can't get involved,' he told her. 'Of course,' she replied. 'Shall I buy us a new eiderdown tomorrow?'

From Bob Geldof, 'Is that It?' 1986

HEATED EXCHANGE

Edward VIII was introduced to Mrs **Wallis Simpson**, in what surely was the great romance of the century, at a winter party at the home of **Lady Furness**. The chat-up lines they used were, as you might expect, classics, though in different ways:

HRH: I suppose you miss central heating in England?

MRS S: (coolly) I would have expected something more original than that from the Prince of Wales!

With that he was hooked, of course. No one had ever dared to put him down like that before and his indebtedness was such that he would have to *prove* to Mrs Simpson at every future opportunity just what a dashing young man-about-town he was.

From Sheilah Graham, 'For Richer, for Poorer', 1975

DRESSING GOWN JACK FLASH

Mick Jagger and **Jerry Hall** met when Mick rang **Bryan Ferry**, Jerry's then fiancé, and invited them along to his concert. Backstage, she recorded in her autobiography: 'Mick was sitting there in his dressing gown and he was much smaller than I'd imagined. There he was, all scrunched down on his knees by the coffee table, and he looked really small and slim and fragile and feminine, somehow, but really sexy and interesting and . . . he sort of scared me with his dressing gown. Do you know what I mean? It was definitely a sexual feeling.' Later they went out to dinner and in the limousine he pressed his knee against hers: 'I could feel the electricity. It was love at first sight.' She also wrote: 'I think big lips are very attractive.' Hundreds of phone calls from Mick then led to the inevitable. He was rebuffed by a jealous Ferry, but the Rolling Stone persisted and contrived for her to sit between **Warren Beatty** and himself at a dinner party. Frantic phone calls then fixed Warren with another girl and Jerry was persuaded to visit Mick's bedroom 'just for a cup of tea'.

From Jerry Hall, 'Tall Tales', 1985

LEADING JOB SITUATIONS FOR GIRLS TO MEET MEN

This list must surely be led by House of Commons secretaries—for influence, power, glory, oneupwomanship etc. Among those in recent years falling for their staff:

Christopher Chope, junior Environment minister—m. 1987 his secretary, **Christo Hutchinson**.

John Wakeham, latterly Leader of the House—m. 1985 (2nd) his civil service secretary, **Alison Ward**.

Nigel Lawson, latterly Chancellor of the Exchequer—m. 1980 (2nd) Commons researcher **Thérèse Medawar**.

Douglas Hurd, latterly Home Secretary—m. 1982 (2nd) **Judy Smart**, secretary to himself and **Sir Geoffrey Howe**.

John Biffen, previously Leader of the House—m. 1979 his secretary, **Sarah Wood**. Not to mention the late **John Stonehouse**, whose secretary, **Sheila Buckley**, fled with him to Australia after he 'did a Reggie Perrin'. And definitely, not to mention **Cecil Parkinson** (I think you just did—Ed).

SOME OTHER USEFUL POSITIONS FOR GIRLS
Air stewardess
Betting shop assistant
Travel courier
Nightclub dancer
Traffic warden

LEADING JOB SITUATIONS FOR MEN TO MEET GIRLS
Ballet teacher
Male model
Sex therapist
Solicitor (all those unhappy divorcées)
Plumber

HE FELL AT HER FEET
Neil and **Glenys Kinnock** met at the 'Freshers Fair' of stalls advertising various societies at Cardiff University. It was Glenys, a former Miss National Savings Beauty Queen, who made the first move, approaching the future Labour leader with the immortal words: 'Are you the man from the Socialist Society?' The meeting led young Neil to plot all week how to win young Miss Glenys Parry at the university union dance the next Saturday night. There was just one problem. He was injured playing rugby during the afternoon and his

injury, compounded by the effect of a couple of pints of beer, led him to swoon and collapse on the dance floor. He was violently sick. It was Glenys, being a chivalrous type of girl, who offered to walk him back to his digs. 'It was a case of me taking him home rather than the other way round,' she said.

> *From Robert Harris, 'The Making of Neil Kinnock', 1984; G. M. F. Drower, 'Neil Kinnock: The Path to Leadership', 1984*

WHERE'S THE ORGY?

John Lennon linked up **Yoko Ono** after the Beatle was persuaded by **Marianne Faithfull**'s husband **John Dunbar** to attend a pop art gallery, the Indica, where according to Dunbar, 'Some of the exhibits resembled an orgy.' There were to be lots of young people lying around in a big bag. The exhibit was entitled: 'Unfinished paintings and objects by Yoko Ono'. When he arrived, the conversation was like a surreal script:

JL: Where's the orgy?

(YO silently hands JL a card reading 'breathe'.)

JL: (panting) You mean like this?

(JL then climbs up a ladder to see ceiling painting which reads: 'Yes'.)

JL: Yes.

(JL then approaches painting entitled 'Hammer a Nail in'.)

JL: Could I hammer a nail into it?

JOHN DUNBAR: Let him hammer a nail in. Who knows, he might buy it.

YO: OK, if you give me five shillings.

JL: OK. I'll give you an imaginary five shillings if you let me hammer an imaginary nail in.

(Fits of laughter from Yoko, who said later: 'It was fantastic! That is what life is all about. I realized that was my own game. Someone was playing the same game as me.')

Yes, that was it folks. She then kept badgering John to back her various *avant garde* exhibitions and projects; she wrote while he was in India visiting the 'Maharoonie', advising him to 'Dance', 'Breathe' and 'Watch all the lights till dawn'. Then one night when wife Cynthia was away he invited her round. They composed 'Two Virgins' between midnight and dawn and then made love.

'It was very beautiful,' he said, even if it wasn't the orgy he was after in the first place.

From the Observer, *21 July 1968;* Daily Express, *12 March 1969; The Rolling Stone Interviews 1981*

3

Best Sweet Nothings from the Dream Factory

As Mills said to Boon said to Barbara Cartland said to John Huston, it is not love so much as the film industry which maketh the world go round. Since so many man and woman hours over the century have been devoted to quenching our insatiable thirst for watching, on the silver screen, others pursuing their sexual quarry, we must ask: what great lovelines have Hollywood provided for us to copy?

Wonderful Romantic Lovelines from the Movies

'Why don't you come up and see me? I'm home every evening.'
Mae West to Cary Grant in 'She Done Him Wrong' (1933). (She never actually said 'Come up and see me sometime'.)

'Why don't you get out of that wet coat and into a dry Martini?'
Robert Benchley to Ginger Rogers in 'The Major and the Minor' (1942)

'There's nothing to be ashamed of. Under this thin veneer of civilization, we're all savages—man, woman, hopelessly enmeshed. We're on a great toboggan. We can't stop it. We can't steer it. It's too late to run. The beguine has begun.'
Tom Ewell to Marilyn Monroe in 'The Seven Year Itch' (1955)

'Mrs Robinson, you're trying to seduce me.
Aren't you?'
*Dustin Hoffman to Anne Bancroft in 'The
Graduate' (1970)*

'Honey, when you smile, it's like the sun
coming up.'
*Clark Gable to Marilyn Monroe in 'The Misfits'
(1961)*

'You need somebody, and I need somebody
too. Could it be you and me, Blanchie?'
*Karl Malden to Vivien Leigh in 'A Streetcar
Named Desire' (1951)*

'Would you be shocked if I put on
something more comfortable?'
*Jean Harlow to Ben Lyon in 'Hell's Angels'
(1930)*

'You need kissing and badly. That's what's
wrong with you. You need kissing—and
often. And by someone who knows how.'
*Clark Gable to Vivien Leigh in 'Gone With the
Wind' (1939)*

'If you want anything, just whistle . . .'
*Lauren Bacall to Humphrey Bogart in 'To Have
and Have Not' (1944)*

'Oh Jerry, don't let's ask for the moon. We
have the stars.'
*Bette Davis to Paul Heinreid in 'Now Voyager'
(1942)*

'Do you see that star?—the brightest one in
the sky. It reminds me of my home. Every
night from my bed I look from my window
and see it shining in the sky. And when I am
away from the Soviet Union I look at the
star and it makes me feel at home.
    From now on every time I see that star it
will remind me of you.'
*Peter Firth and Alexandra Pigg in 'Letter to
Brezhnev' (1985)*

'And you. What do *you* dream about?'
Apollonia to Prince in 'Purple Rain' (1985)

Liberating Sexual Suggestions from the Cinema

'Let me outline the following procedure. As soon as the music starts you will begin removing your clothing. As you remove each article I will throw on this table a bill of the denomination of 15, 10 or 20 dollars depending entirely on my fancy which you will not bother to calculate. You follow me? All right, on the table, miss, on the table!'

J. Arthur Conrad to Lynn Redgrave in 'The Happy Hooker' *(1975)*

'Do you like it?'

Marlon Brando to Maria Schneider in 'Last Tango in Paris' *(1972)*

'Smells good in here today.'

Jack Nicholson to Jessica Lange just before the 'kitchen table' sequence in 'The Postman Always Rings Twice' *(1981)*

'You're a beautiful woman but you lead such a sheltered life. It's all there in your eyes . . . You can tell everything in a woman's eyes. You're not getting enough.'

Cliff Gorman to Jill Clayburgh in 'An Unmarried Woman' *(1978)*

'Take me to your loft, Charlie.'

Jill Clayburgh to Cliff Gorman in 'An Unmarried Woman' *(1978)*

'You know, there are three things we could do right now: you could call a taxi and go home or we could go on walking and I could lecture you on the meaning of modern art, or we could go to my place and thoroughly enjoy each other.'

Alan Bates to Jill Clayburgh in 'An Unmarried Woman' *(1978)*

'Are you a virgin? Fortunately you're talking to a man who specializes in such diseases.'

Doug Fisher to Natalie Ogle in 'The Stud' *(1978)*

'The joystick is a sensitive piece of equipment. It has to be handled carefully.'
Richard Oldfield to Koo Stark in 'Emily' *(1976)*

'I'd like to be smothered by you.'
Jack Nicholson to Anne-Margaret in 'Carnal Knowledge' *(1971)*

Chat-up Line

Perhaps the most celebrated (and least elaborate) chat-up lines of history came in a written exchange between the **Prince de Joinville** and the great French actress **Rachel**. After seeing her act, he sent her a note, reading: '*Ou? Quand? Combien?*' (Where, when, how much?'), to which, to his great pleasure, he received an almost instantaneous response: '*Chez toi. Ce soir. Pour Rien.*' ('Your place, tonight, for nothing.')

Best Comic Chat-up Lines from Hollywood

'Oh, why can't we break away from all this, just you and I, and lodge with my fleas in the hills? I mean, flee to my lodge in the hills.'
Groucho Marx to Thelma Todd in 'Monkey Business' *(1931)*

'I don't know how to kiss or I would kiss you. Where do the noses go?'
Ingrid Bergman to Gary Cooper in 'For Whom the Bell Tolls' *(1943)*

'I get a nice, warm feeling being near you, Ma'am. It's like being around a pot-bellied stove in the morning.'
Rock Hudson to Doris Day in 'Pillow Talk' *(1958)*

'Your eyes shine like the pants of my blue serge suit.'
Groucho Marx in 'The Cocoanuts' *(1929)*

'I could dance with you until the cows come home. On second thoughts I'll dance with the cows and you come home.'
Groucho Marx in 'Animal Crackers' *(1930)*

'Marry me and I'll never look at another horse.'
Groucho Marx in 'A Day at the Races' *(1937)*

'You're what Grammy Hall would call a real Jew.'
Diane Keaton to Woody Allen in 'Annie Hall' *(1977)*

'Hump or death. You've got ten seconds to make up your mind.'
Mel Brooks to Pamela Stephenson in 'History of the World Part I' *(1981)*

'I gotta learn to do it without the dress.'
Dustin Hoffman to Jessica Lange in 'Tootsie' *(1985)*

'Did you think you would spend the night?'
'Can't, thanks.'
Meryl Streep and Robert Redford in 'Out of Africa' *(1986)*

'Take me!'
'Take you where?'
Sean Young and Peter Strauss in 'Tender is the Night' *(1986 TV movie)*

'We'd better kiss soon—we're coming to The End.'
Mel Brooks to Pamela Stephenson in 'History of the World Part I' *(1981)*

4

Learning from the Rich and Famous

'Explain yourself,' said **Princess Margaret** on meeting a young man called **Roddy Llewellyn** at **Colin Tennant**'s home in Scotland. 'Bring on that boy!' said **Britt Ekland** on spying a good-looking young Spaniard she met in a disco in Marbella.

The modern sophisticate can learn much from observing the courtship habits of the rich and famous.

Actor **Patrick Duffy**, Bobby Ewing of *Dallas*, offered this explanation of how he met his wife, **Carlyn**:

'There were five dancers in the company so I thought I'd work my way through them starting on the left. Carlyn was the first on the left and we fell head over heels in love.'

Many times, of course, it's the woman who makes the first move. Model **Patti D'Arbanville** spotted Hollywood's hottest property in designer pants, *Miami Vice* star **Don Johnson**, in a bar, when she was having dinner. Boldly she marched up to him and asked: 'How many times have you been married?' When he told her three, she replied: 'Welcome to number four!' They spent the next eight days together in bed.

One of the great dynastic marriages of political history came when **Ferdinand Marcos** became infatuated with a young woman called **Imelda** who had watched him speak in the Philippines Congress. The highlight of his whirlwind courtship was a visit to a private bank vault, where he showed her the piles of US currency he had amassed. They wed eleven days later.

According to American model **Patricia Burke** in the *Sun* in December, 1986, A-ha star **Morten Haarket** had a unique way of dealing with eager groupies: he would sit on the end of the bed with them and lecture them for hours on God and moral values. 'Come to bed for a Bible lesson,' paraphrased the *Sun*'s headline writer, of this natty line in chat. 'Did you hear the parable of the virgins?'

One does, however, seem to have a little more of a pick of the opposite sex if you are a showbiz star. **Jimmy Savile** went down in the quotation books for 'I never ever ring a girl up. Girls have to ring me. That, to me, is the fairest way of going on.' While *Dallas* star **Larry Hagman** blamed an early girlfriend for setting him off on a one-time chain smoking spiral:

'I was necking with a girl when I was fourteen and she said she would let me

take liberties if I tried a cigarette.'

It has been suggested that modern sophisticates should try to emulate the stars. American sexologists Masters and Johnson recommended that male patients watch the movie *Crocodile Dundee* to master the art of wooing women subtly. We will remain agnostic after a four-X response from Mr Dundee, alias Aussie comedian **Paul Hogan**, that the two distinguished medics were 'off the planet'. He said: 'It cracked me up. Nowhere in the movie does my rough-hewn character in his croc-toothed hat say anything as gushing as "You look nice".'

My own favourite first approach comes from the literary world, with this poetic plea from a character called Boris Adrian in *Blue Movie* by **Terry Southern**:

'You know . . . the thing that *really* attracted me to you,' he began quietly, as though thinking aloud to himself, 'the thing I find really . . . *beautiful,*

Norman Collier
Comedian

Favourite chat-up line

I couldn't pull a muscle, let alone pull a bird. I was always a wallflower. I remember how I met the wife. She wore suede shoes—one swayed one way, one the other. She was knock-kneed to keep her stockings up. A policeman stopped me and said: 'I've come to deal with the accident.'

Best lines tried on me

When they're interested, they *lean* on you.

'Ere, come 'ere, Norman, give us a kiss.' I try to avoid it when I can. Perhaps a gas mask would be the answer. The worst are Welsh women. They seem to be a bit hot. I was once getting washed in what passed for a dressing-room at a club—I only had a towel round me— when a large Welsh woman with big boobs appeared and shouted: 'Oooh. Ooooh!! He's got some hairs on his chest.' She then picked me up bodily and tried to get the towel off me. Imagine, this big, Welsh woman. She had such strong arms she nearly crushed me. I've never been so frightened in my life.

maybe even *uniquely beautiful* in you, at least for today—and I say this with all humility and respect, because I know you must have other qualities, and I recognize that it may be some kind of weakness in myself—not weakness exactly, but still not the sort of thing I'd like to be able to say, the sort of thing I

imagine you'd like to hear . . . but the thing that makes you really . . . *exceptional*—well, I mean to me, anyway . . . is your ass.'

These days, if you're not into rolypolygrams or electronic mail Valentines a number of visual aids are available to smooth the garden path of the art of romance. From America comes the 'flirt handkerchief' which you can drop to be picked up. (Yes, you and the handkerchief). It has, of course, your name and phone number discreetly emblazoned thereupon. To help the electricity between you, in 1984 in France they came up with 'le Flashing', a singles device about the size of a pack of cigarettes. It sends out a signal to other 'le Flashing' users indicating that you have a few kilowatts of passion to spare. ('Let me take you ohm'.) Though perhaps most useful in the Aids-conscious eighties came in 1985 from Denver, Colorado, to give you protection against the man or woman who has everything. It is a plastic credit card indicating that the bearer has successfully passed tests for twenty-three sexually transmitted diseases.

New York, of course, is the home of 'swinging singles'. (A singles convention at Madison Square Garden attracted 32,000). Recent years have seen no end of treatises on 'Manhattan man-eaters' who lurk in bars, in basement launderettes and at health clubs. Then, of course, they club poor males on the head and whisk them to the altar, or at least to bed where they are served up with lashings of whipped cream or olive oil.

Top New York predatory-girl chat-up lines, according to an article in the *Sun* in March 1985 ('They know we are after their bodies') were:

1 Could you pass me the peanuts and your phone number?
2 Come up and see my bell bars;
3 I'm gay but maybe you could convert me; and
4 I think you'd make a wonderful father.

Determined females (and males!) have always been a problem for show business and sports stars, of course, like:

Pop idol **Paul King**, who received an envelope containing the key to a chastity belt and a message: 'Keep this safe, it's yours to use whenever you want.'

Eddie Large
Comedian

Worst chat-up line

'Do you mind looking after the keys to my Porsche?' Actually it was a mini van. Neither of us had a car in those days. 'Me car's in the garage,' we had to tell them.

Best line used on me

At the Royal at Bournemouth I ran into a party of pensioners. One of them asked me to sign her pot leg. It was the best chat-up line I'd ever had. She just swung it up and handed it to me. I've heard of a 'legover' but that was ridiculous!

South African tennis star **Eddie** (not the Eagle) **Edwards**, who advised a persistent admirer who collared him in the presence of his girlfriend to 'go away', only to be told:

'My friend's house is free for a couple of hours. We could really have a nice time.'

TV presenter **Michael Aspel**, who had an attractive young female fan throw herself across the bonnet of his car.

Also: Treasure Hunt star **Anneka Rice**, who received a train ticket to the Isle of Wight and the summons: 'I have booked a hotel for the weekend of the 25th, I'll join you there.'

Songster **Cliff Richard**, who was cornered by a girl fan proclaiming 'God has sent me to you.'

Actor **Paul Usher** (Barry Grant of *Brookside*), who received a message exhorting: 'My husband's out at work from 9 am to 5 pm. Scratch your nose before the first commercial break if you're interested.'

Debbi Peterson of The Bangles received a letter saying: 'Come over and I'll fix you spaghetti and give you some cheap wine and we'll have a good time and I'll kiss your neck'. And **Selina Scott**, according to Rita Carter's book, *Fan Mail*, got this missive: 'I'd like to marry you, please, though I think to be fair to you it would be a good idea if we met first.'

Perhaps the best-ever run-down of aggressive sexual technique came from **Woody Allen**. It ran thus:

'First find a girl. Then lean her against something soft. Another girl will do. Third put on the most seductive recording you can find of "Sheep May Safely Graze". Last, show her your collection of post-Impressionist chopped liver. That should do it. For the first twenty-five years of my life I chased girls and they all had headaches. Now it is much easier when I pursue them. They don't get headaches quickly—but I do.'

Dave Barrett
Commercial radio DJ

Worst chat-up lines
'Do you know your dress matches my sheets back home?'
'You look different to how you sound on the radio. I'm not sure I will listen to you anymore, but you can buy me a drink.'
'Give me the kiss of life.'

5

Essential Kit for the Committed Match-Player

Make no mistake, just as you have to 'dress for success', your chances will be much enhanced in the personal introduction stakes if you prepare about your person a few handy aids (of the non-chiselled government leaflet variety).

DON'T take out with you:

A watch (then you've got lots of excuses for asking others the time);

A calculator (then you can ask others to do your adding up);

A specific gravity device for measuring the strength of beer (really boring).

DO however carry at all times possible:

A cigarette lighter. You don't have to smoke yourself. But the well-practised seductive lunge with the flint at the right moment has sparked off many beautiful friendships. Make sure you know the difficult bit, how to flick off the top and light the thing, by the way.

A scarf, gloves, handkerchief or flat cap. To leave behind 'accidentally' or drop casually for others to pick up. (But make sure you use inexpensive items, there are so many kleptomaniacs around these days).

A small bag or emblem (or pendant or ankle chain). This is the most cunning, sure-fire way of focusing eyes on you. What's that? Where did you get it? Is it real diamante? Most important of all, it should have a tiny, barely legible inscription (then targets must come as close as close can be to read it). This should not be hackneyed or political ('I'm a virgin, this is a very old badge,' 'This is a *Sun*-free zone', etc.) but instead should be tantalizing and cryptic: 'The last star always sleeps before dawn', 'Boris and Delilah send their commiserations', 'More of the swing and less of the wiggle'.

What's it mean? Why, you leave *them* to work it out. Actually the inscription means absolutely nothing but will lead you into some very interesting conversations. Those you don't like are meanwhile repulsed by the explanation, 'It means I'm an *SM* gay', 'It means I've got herpes', etc. (always chancing to luck that's not what they are and are trawling around for the same).

A £50 note. Only one. This gives you the impression of being a high roller. It also means your target will more than likely say, oh, don't bother to break into that, allow me . . .

A 40-function official boy scout camp knife (most essential functions being a corkscrew, bottle opener and proboscis for removing stones from horses' hooves). This will allow you to outperform all competitors at those awkward moments when no one can uncork the wine, decant the Guinness, dissect the Stilton. You'll be an instant hero/heroine.

A fake symbol of athletic prowess. This can be as a slogan on a T-shirt, badge on a jumper, lettering on a travel bag, etc. The best will attempt to indicate the membership of a small élite unit, e.g. '**XXXV** Olympiad British National Superbowl Squad', 'World Sunflower Seed Eating Champion, 1989,' 'Chelsea FC goalscorer this season'. The idea is to convey glamour, superfitness and portray you as a fitness/sex maniac.

A small packet of cocktail sticks. This useful prop doubles to offer suggestively to likely targets (1) if your host/hostess is too mean to put them out with the olives and cocktail onions; and (2) if you see a target standing awkwardly with a hand in their mouth, gurgling: 'I've got something stuck in my teeth.'

Contact lenses (real or imaginary). There is nothing more guaranteed to get people mingling successfully (scrambling on the floor with heads, and therefore lips, pressured close) than to cry: 'I've lost one of my contact lenses. Can everybody help me look for it?' No, of course you don't really have to wear them!

A roll of aluminium foil or plastic freezer

bags. For another vital moment, when your hostess/host decides to pack up what's left of the grub having remembered she/he has got nothing at all for Sunday lunch. This act of foresight, charm and generosity is most times rewarded with an invitation to stay the night.

OPTIONAL EXTRAS for the really adventurous include:
Pocket phone books in fifteen languages;
A mini fire extinguisher;
A legal aid handbook;
A monkey wrench (to deal with plumbing malfunctions);
Jump start leads;
A bottle of disinfectant or carpet cleaner;
A puncture repair outfit; and
A rubber inflatable dinghy.

But remember, you will need either a large briefcase, or handbag or some pretty deep pockets to deploy the complete kit!

6

Be My Valentine

Pigbum loves Moo the Monk—true. Snuggles is wanted for cuddles by Smarty Underpants. Monkey Face adores Smelly more than ever. Pongiwumps wants to get it together with Wilhelmina Wombat. Emperor Chop Suey has hot stuff in store for Madam Flashbang (a quick wallop?).

The genteel, ornate, and chastely Victorian world of traditional Valentine's Day cards has been much eclipsed in recent years by a growing spectator sport: the one- line greetings insertion in a national newspaper. Sometimes rude, more often than not quite incomprehensible, occasionally hinting at secret and forbidden fruit-gathering, the Valentine's Day ads are chat-up lines in themselves.

So among the Darling Skewers ('I'm really stuck on you—Kebab'); the Poohfaces ('Hedgepig loves you, bedoyng, bedoyng, bedoyng'); not to mention Warthogs loving Rhinoceroses ('even though it's physically impossible'), this book—assuming A. A. Milne is not on the warpath for royalties—gives you the best of Valentine's Day columns of recent memory.

Absolutely Romantic Valentine Messages

We shall start by keeping it entirely clean with the most soppy—sorry, inventively romantic—lines to melt anyone's heart.

DEAREST SUSAN. My love for you has no

bounds and your love provides the glow that lights my soul.

From the Guardian, *1986*

PEBBLES. I love you today more than yesterday but not as much as tomorrow.

From the Daily Mirror, *1986*

Let me be the song in your heart. Your Valentine.

From The Times, *1985*

I left my heart at Seven Wells. It's there my own true lover dwells.

From The Times, *1985*

JENNY. Not quite your name in lights but in my heart, always.

From The Times, *1985*

LYN, you are as precious to me as the air I breathe.

From The Times, *1985*

Valentine Lovers Who Said it in Verse

There's no day like February 14th for bringing out the budding Wordsworths among us.
ROSES ARE RED
Violets are blue
Tigger and Eeyore
And Bungle love you.
PS: So did Pooh but it didn't fit.

From the Guardian, *1985*

YOU MOVE with style, grace so light,
Like Wordsworth's *Phantom of Delight*.

From The Times, *1985*

BEV: Roses are red, violets are blue, all I need is my blow-up doll and you.

From the Sunday Telegraph, *1988*

TO ETH
Valentine, Valentine,
Over the river,
When I kill the pig,
I'll throw you its liver.

From the Guardian, *1986*

FATTY POO:
I wish I was a nice warm towel
Hanging on your bath
And when I saw your lovely bod
I know I'd laugh and laugh.

From the Sun, *1986*

I LOVE DEE, DEE, Georgie's fat,
Picky's off his rocker, so that's that.

From The Times, *1985*

Crazy Valentine's Day Greetings

Most of the Valentine's Day ads are, of course, just plain amazing.
DEAR S. . .bag. Please be my Valentine—Dustbin.

From the Guardian, *1985*

JANE—Love is filling in skips on a Saturday afternoon. All my love—Knackered.

From the Guardian, *1985*

MOUSETOES. Wishing you a happy birthday and Fifty Large Ducky bumps. Love light fingers.

From the Daily Telegraph, *1986*

WEDGIE seeks Liz for funloving political relationship.

From the Guardian, *1986*

KNOCKERFLOP. I love you. From your little Piranha.

From the Daily Mail, *1984*

TO THE YETI—I LOVE YOU ALWAYS. The Blob.

From the Guardian, *1986*

BROCK BADGER loves his nibbly twiglet. Yum, Yum, Yum.

From the Guardian, *1985*

DEAR GRAVY be my Oxo tonight; your bald meat ball.

From The Times, *1985*

MICHELE. Diddums Koochie Oochie koo Ickle Nicky Wicky Poo.

From The Times, *1985*

BEAUTIFUL Bootsy Buster supertech, our love is the core of my life. Toady.

From the Daily Telegraph, *1986*

PLODDY. Animal misses her Pig. Hope you trot home soon. From Smelly Feet Linda.

From the Daily Mirror, *1986*

TO TURD—copious love and affection now and forever from your Cochon.

From the Guardian, *1986*

TO THE MAN WITH STILE! I have always had a soft spot for boring old farts.

From the Guardian, *1986*

7

Winning Hearts, Minds (and Bodies) in One Devastating Breath

Like cooking steak, visiting the turf accountants or fishing for salmon, it cannot be stressed too loftily that there is no one formula for making your target melt uncontrollably into your arms. Use the approach (or approaches) which come most naturally. *Observe* your victim and work out which method they are most likely to respond to.

The Flash, Smooth Approach

Still tops in the discos, the idea is to convey a mixture of wealth, warmth and suspense with the hidden promise of a lifetime's excitement to come. The hint is of candlelight dinners, jet hops to Rio and romantic arrivals at expensive star haunts in a private jet, or at least a crumbling old Porsche.

You'll need to keep your hair perfectly in place, wear designer clothes and practise every move in front of a mirror night and day.

Advantages: Proven over centuries. It looks good, makes you feel good, and . . .

Disadvantages: You'll probably be thought something of a wally. You'll have to lie through your teeth. And worst of all, it will cost you a large amount of money.

Heroes and heroines: Chris Quinten.

Musical accompaniment: Michael Jackson; Tom Jones; Terence Trent D'Arby.

EXAMPLES
Come on, snake, let's wiggle.
I'm young an' single an' I love to mingle.

35

You know they say diamonds are a girl's best friend? Well, that was before I came along.

I'm a lovehunter sniffing at your door.

I'm an electric gypsy and I shoot to thrill.

I collect telephone ringing tones and I'm told yours is a hot number.

I'm a duvet tester by trade. Have you been tested yet?

Would you like to try some of my special therapy? It'll make us both feel better.

If I told you I were a millionaire, would you lie to me too?

The Rough and Ready Approach

Either you're a macho no-nonsense man or a determined, no-nonsense girl. Your natural inclination is to march right in there, and give it to them straight. At its least sophisticated, it's really saying: 'Do you or don't you?' At its more subtle, it's still 'Do you or don't you?'

Tony Blackburn
Disc jockey

Favourite chat-up lines
'What are you doing for the rest of your life?'
Pulls out a thermometer—takes own temperature—sees it's normal and then says: 'I'm OK, I can take you out tonight!'

Worst chat-up lines
'If I said you had a nice figure, would you hold it against me?'
'You're like a department store—something on every floor.'

Personal recipe for attracting the opposite sex
I sit on a chair in a wine bar, then seductively pull up one trouser leg to show the top of my sock. It drives them mad with desire.

Many, of course, welcome this laying on the line. It's for disciples of the old adage: 'Treat 'em mean, and keep 'em keen.'

Advantages: Some people love the rugged approach. You get a quick answer one way or the other. Having started out asking for a lot in return for very little, you won't have to waste time paying for candlelit dinners.

Disadvantages: You burn all your boats straight away. The standard of those accepting may not be too high. For every success, you'll have three or four humiliating failures. You're in much greater danger from rival suitors than if you had been polite. Can you keep it up?

Heroes and heroines: Oliver Reed; Clint Eastwood; Joan Collins; Madonna.

Musical accompaniment: Ravel's *Bolero*; Stravinsky's *Rite of Spring*; anything by the Beastie Boys.

EXAMPLES

You've obviously got a stiff neck—I'm great at massage.

The next time you take a shower, can I dry you off?

Come a little closer. Well, move a little closer anyway.

Do you talk dirty, or just look as if you do?

You could be the most fun I had without laughing.

They call me JCB—I always make the earth move.

I'm a bit like an old Cortina. I need lots of touching up.

They call me Air Canada—because I'm so good, no one wants to get off.

Let's pretend it's bayonet practice and hit the sack.

Him to her: I'm Captain Kirk. How's about letting me boldly go where no man's gone before?

If I took my clothes off, would you hold it right there?

Her to him: Go on, I'll respect you in the morning.

You must have something very interesting down there the way you're always standing with your hands in your pockets.

Michael Groth
TV presenter

Favourite chat-up line
'I bet you've got the kind of toenails that curl inwards, haven't you?' (This was tried on me, to great effect.)
Worst chat-up line
'Do you come here often?'

The Romantic Approach

If you believe the best of the opposite sex have to be wooed and won, then this is the most spectacular, satisfying—though also agonizing—way to go about it. You'll need to follow up with countless bottles of champagne, flowers, Valentines and boxes of chocolates, of course. But take pride in the delicacy of it all.

Advantages: Played right, it looks simply stunning. It's every girl's dream—and many a man's too.

Disadvantages: It's a bit old hat. They might laugh in your face. It's not merely costly in the long run, but time-consuming too.

Heroes and heroines: Valentino; Clark Gable; Richard Gere; Lesley Anne Down; Victoria Principal; Barbara Cartland.

Musical accompaniment: Prokofiev's *Romeo and Juliet*; Rachmaninov; The Housemartins; Max Bygraves.

Using Flattery

Flattery will get you many places, but not *quite* everywhere. The skill is using it sincerely, without which you might as well go home and play with your Scalextric/Cabbage Patch doll/cyclotron/home computer. Otherwise, of course, it's absolutely wonderful, marvellous, fantastic.

Go on then, approach the best-looking target in the place. But look them straight in the eye and *never*, never laugh. What a wonderful vision! What style! Absolutely marvellous . . .

Advantages: It is the simplest way of making sure someone falls for you.

Don Maclean
Comedian

Favourite chat-up line
'Madam, I am an insect specialist. How would you like to see the inside of a fly?'

Worst chat-up lines
I was always very polite. Somewhere like the Locarno in Birmingham I would approach a girl and say: 'Could I have this dance, please?' I really like some of the put downs:
(Brummie accent) 'Are you talking to me or chewing a brick?'
'Could I have the last dance?'
—'You're already having it.'
Young fellow to sophisticated woman of 18½: 'Could I have this dance?'
—'I wouldn't dance with a baby.'—
'Oh, sorry—I didn't realize you were in that condition.'

Disadvantages: It's difficult to carry off. It's monumentally easy to blow it.
Heroes and heroines: Bob Monkhouse; Larry Hagman; Gloria Hunniford.
Musical accompaniment: Greensleeves; anything by Mel and Kim.

EXAMPLES
The thing I noticed about you straight away is that you have a mind.
When I see you I feel like bursting into applause.
If you were caviar you'd be Beluga.
I've never seen so much style outside of the Ritz.
Can you be real or have you walked out of some Paris fashion magazine?
The last time anyone looked as stunning as you—I was only dreaming.
There is one thing in the world I would love to be—your pillow.
Her to him: I'm going to call you Gelatin. You could turn any girl to jelly.
Him to her: You're the most perfect living thing I've seen. It's a pity Da Vinci isn't still

alive so he could paint you. (It could be worse, it could be Rubens!)

I think you're a man-trap: I'd like to fall in right away.

Paul Coia
TV *presenter*

Favourite chat-up line

'I'm compiling a telephone directory and would like to include your number.'

Best lines tried on me

The best ones are the ones that make you laugh. A girl once told me that I had the 'skin of a peach'. As I preened, she continued: 'A football peetch.' Another told me that I should have been born in the Dark Ages. 'You look lousy in the light!' she finished.

The Little Boy (or Girl) Lost Approach

This well-tried and trusted tactical ploy relies on appealing to your target's maternal (or paternal) instincts. Stand in a corner. Look sultry. Look shy. Lost. Sulk. Roll off the tongue platitudes like 'What's it all about?', 'Nobody cares a dot for me', 'Just call me little Cinders' and 'I don't know who's going to take me to the party.'

This will either make you violently unpopular as a whingeing liability or get you noticed as 'not one of the crowd' to the extent that every shoulder of the opposite sex around will be thrust in your face to cry on.

Advantages: It's not too hard on the vocal chords. It must be hard to resist the temptation to smile or laugh every so often.

Disadvantages: People do tire eventually of those who take more than they give. You could become a permanent wallflower.

Heroes and heroines: Rodney in *Only Fools and Horses*; Gail in *Coronation Street*.

Musical accompaniment: Leonard Cohen; Beethoven; funeral marches; anything mournful.

EXAMPLES

Could you please take pity on a poor downtrodden millionaire/BMW owner/ racing yacht owner.

My gas is off. Can I come round to your place to cook my toast?

My electricity is off. Can I come round to play my U2 tapes?

My heating's off. Can I come round to your place for a bath?

I don't suppose you could take in a poor waif and stray for the night.

Most girls I know eat men for breakfast. But I can tell you're a vegetarian.

You look so brainy chatting over there! You're not going to give me an IQ test are you?

You don't have to believe me, but I'm a famous rock star recovering from being dried out. I can't tell you my name.

Him to her: Where have you been all my wife?

The Insulting Approach

This extremely tactical ploy is perhaps the greatest weapon in the armoury of the serious student of the chat-up technique: and it can yield the best dividends. Why do you hear so often that such-and-such won the heart of so-and-so after deeply wounding him/her with words? The answer is psychology. What you are doing when you tell someone 'you're ugly' is unleashing a chain response which makes them then seek to prove that, of course, they're not. So they will chase you around until they've proved otherwise to their satisfaction. So, paradoxically, with insult rather than flattery, you have cemented a lasting relationship.

Oh yes: one simple courtesy—having done the dirty, you have to have the good grace to listen to their replies!

Advantages: Sets up a semi-permanent bond between you. You can be clever with it so you retain the advantage until the target makes the next move.

Disadvantages: They might want their own back so badly, they hit you, or worse, get their fathers, brothers, the boys, etc. to do it.

Heroes and heroines: Bernard Manning; Dame Edna Everage; Kate Adie; Ben Elton; Harry Cross in *Brookside*.

Musical accompaniment: Anything by Max Boyce, Billy Connolly or Alexei Sayle.

EXAMPLES

I don't know what you'll look like tomorrow, but in the dark you're OK.

You must have been a beautiful puppy. No I didn't say baby—I said puppy.

Who designed your clothes—British Steel?

Who did the retread on your lips—Goodyear?

You look lovely tonight—was it an accident?

If I pinched your bottom, would I get done for grand larceny?

Did you say something or was that the fire alarm?

Is that your face I see reflected in your shoes, or have you stood in something nasty?

I saw you open your mouth. Are you expecting visitors?

Her to him:

Do you believe in fairies or do you just look like one?

Do you stick the hairs on your chest individually or all at once?

If I kiss you, would you turn into a prince? You certainly look like a prize toad.

Him to her:

Me Tarzan, you plain.

Are you fluttering your eyelashes or is there a plane coming in to land?

(Peering down cleavage) I love these backless dresses.

That's a very good designer stubble you've got on your chin.

The Game Play Approach

This involves deliberately planting a stock phrase or saying and inviting a reply. If they fall for the trap *or* know the proper answer, you'll be laughing all the way to—well, wherever.

Advantages: You will immediately tell if you are on the same wavelength. It's a quick way to begin a warm, loving relationship.

Disadvantages: They might resent being used as a stooge. They might have a better answer up their sleeves.

Heroes and heroines: Paul Daniels; Sue Lawley; Matthew Corbett; Rodney and Del Boy.

More Restrained Chat-up Lines for the Aids-obsessed Eighties and Nineties

'Hi there, pure little rich girl.'

'Your condominium or mine?'

'I hope you're keeping something under wraps for later.'

'Bet I'm purer than you are.'

'Are you on holiday or are you here for an Aids test?'

'Do you believe in sex before the 93rd date?'

'How would you like to help me curl up with the latest anti-Aids book?'

(Pointing to self) 'Rich man, pure man.'

'I wouldn't sleep with any old Tom, Dick or Harry these days . . . now a Samantha, that's a different story.'

'I've got a banker friend who's into safe sex—every lunchtime in the vault with his secretary.'

'The initials S-E-X never had the same magic as, say, G-t-i in any case.'

'I didn't recognize you without your condom on.'

'Sex could never beat a good game of Scrabble anyhow.'

Musical accompaniment: Vaudeville; drum rolls and whoopee whistles.

EXAMPLES

What's Brazil famous for?

I don't know.

Coffee—at my place.

Can I drive you home?

Have you a car?

No, a whip!

I got the hops for you babe.

Don't you mean 'hots'?

No, I'm a beer drinker.

Do you know the difference between sex and conversation?
Er . . . no . . .
Lie down and I'll explain.

Would you like to see my powdered rhino horn. It's a great aphrodisiac.
Oh, really? Well, yes.
I'll just go to the bathroom and powder it then.

Some of the traditional responses you should know:
Excuse me, I'm trying to get rid of this fellah/girl who's been trying to chat me up. Can I pretend I'm with you?
Correct answer: Why pretend?

You're OK, but I'm afraid I don't date anyone over the age of twenty four.
Correct answer: Neither do I.

I've got a candle burning inside me for you.
Correct answer: That must hurt quite a bit.

If you're going to say no, say it now before I spend all my money on you.
Correct answer: No.

Would you like to see my brand-new Rolls?
Correct answer: Oh, so you're a baker's boy then?

Tell me, what do I have to give you to get a kiss?
Correct answer: Chloroform.

The No-effort, No-expense Approach

Finally, there's the sweetest pick-up of all: the dramatic rescue, or non-chat-up. In this you listen intently to a rival's spiel, elbow aside whoever has been laying it on thick, then whisk off your target, saying: 'I've never heard such a pathetic chat-up routine in my life.'

8

Best Celebrity Come Hithers

As we have said, modern sophisticates seeking divine guidance to dazzle and enthral can do no better than look to the stars.

'Sorry, I didn't quite catch your name . . .' This was the stunning line used by **'Bungalow' Bill Wiggins** on meeting on a blind date one of the most famous women in the world, **Joan Collins**. She liked it, falling about in helpless laughter at the preposterous thought that anyone could fail to recognize her. Yes, it was a genuine flash of wit from 'Bungalow' Bill. He said: 'I'm no great *Dynasty* fan but even I recognized *the* Joan Collins.' He had been invited to a lunch party by friend **Ned Ryan** on the promise of meeting 'an unmarried 23-year-old blonde multi-millionairess'. He confessed that on meeting his blind date he was 'left gasping'. (Well, she is brunette and 31 years older for a start.) Nevertheless, the couple hit it off and became a fully fledged show business partnership after she cemented things with a pretty good return chat-up line: 'I'm not doing anything tomorrow. Perhaps you'd like to take me to dinner.' Alexis herself couldn't have done better.

From the Sun, *16 June 1987*

'Say "terrified". No, say "tissue". Now say "terrified tissue". Faster.' This bizarre routine was **Cary Grant**'s favourite way of bewitching air hostesses, according to biographers. With enough practice the girl would find herself gushing 'Care if I kiss you'—and blushing for all she was worth.

From William Currie McIntosh and William Weaver, 'The Private Cary Grant' 1983

'Mind if I curl up in your lap right now?'
Jimmy Dean's favourite technique was
based on the premise that 'all women want
to mother you. Give them a chance and
before you know it you're home free.'
Favouring older women, the immortal
screen rocker used to simply curl up in their
lap and let them stroke his hair. He claimed
it never failed.

From Irving Wallace, 'The Intimate Sex Lives
of Famous People', *1981*

**'I don't believe in women accountants.
And why are you late?'** These macho
words were the first spoken by her new boss
to a new recruit called **Edwina. Raymond
Currie** later married her, of course. He was
probably the only man to dare speak to her
like that!

From the Guardian, *25 October 1983*

'Can I borrow some glue?' The amazing
stammered chat-up line comes from the man
who, on TV at least, comes across as the
all-time champ—**Paul Nicholas**, alias

Steve Colman
Commercial radio DJ

Favourite chat-up line
'Can I have your autograph, please?
Someone as beautiful as you must be
an actress.'
Best line tried on me
'My telephone is out of order. Can I
take down your number so that I can
ask my friends to call you to take a
message for me?'

Vince Pinner of *Just Good Friends*. He tells how
he took a fancy to the girl who was to become
his wife, **Linzi Jennings**, when she moved
into the flat below. 'After weeks and weeks of
fancying her in silence I said to myself:
"Right! Tonight's the night—it's now or
never." ' But when she opened the door his
nerve deserted him. Hence the sticky question.

From Weekend, *27 October 1985*

'I love the feel of your leather trousers.'
This was the slightly cheeky line used by
former World Champion grand prix driver
James Hunt on model **Liz Hoad** after they
met on a blind date (he had just split with
long-time girlfriend **Jane** 'Hottie' **Birbeck**).
She raved about how romantic he was,
despite a passion for making love to
Meatloaf tapes. She said they both shared
the same sense of humour 'and with James,
nothing was serious'.

From the News of the World, *15 December 1985*

**'I would like to plop something down
your little hole in D-flat major.'** This
inventive musical composition was the work
of **Frederic François Chopin**, aired in a
letter to his pupil **Countess Delfina
Potocka**.

From Irving Wallace, 'The Intimate Sex Lives
of Famous People', *1981*

How Famous Rock and Pop Couples First Met

Howard Jones and his wife **Jan** met
tinkling on the ivories. He was her piano
teacher, to be precise. Although only
thirteen at the time, she described it as 'love
at first sight' and admitted it was Howard
she was interested in, not the pianoforte,
though he did teach her up to Grade III
standard. He ungraciously let it be known
'She's good at the piano but her singing is
awful.'

From the Daily Express, *14 March 1985;*
Evening Standard, *13 July 1984*

Bruce Springsteen and **Juliane Phillips**
met in a hot and crowded room behind stage
at the Los Angeles sports arena in October
1984. 'I had been invited to the show by a
friend and nearly didn't go,' she said. 'I had
no idea that I was going to meet him but in
the intermission we were introduced. The
first thing he said to me was "Will you

Chris Tarrant
Disc jockey and TV performer
('Through the Keyhole')

Favourite chat-up line
(One I overheard). A bloke in Hastings to a girl in a seaside club . . . 'Hallo, I'm Dave . . . This is all a bit embarrassing. I've been plucking up courage to buy you a drink all evening; unfortunately I've just been outside, my Porsche has been stolen with all my money in. Perhaps you'd like to buy me a drink to get us both off on the right foot.'

Worst chat-up lines
(Worst from a lady): 'D'you mind if we go home to my house? There's something terribly wrong with my leg tops.'
(Worst from a man): A bloke to a complete stranger in a pub in Coventry: 'Hi there, Pretty Polly . . . why don't you stop mentally undressing me and experience the real thing. . . ?' The girl threw a drink at him and walked out.

marry me?" No, I'm just kidding; he was very polite.' Juliane was invited to a private dinner party afterwards and said: 'I guess we hit it off.'

From the Sun, *17 October 1986*

Simon Le Bon met wife **Yasmin** after he saw a photo of the top model and asked his manager to ring her up. 'It was the first time I'd ever done that,' he said, 'though I know that some stars like **Rod Stewart** do it all the time.' Soon the couple were seen necking in all London's top night clubs which led friends of Simon to joke: 'It was love at first bite.' He said: 'We met on a blind date and discovered after a bottle of Scotch that we liked each other.'

From the Daily Mirror, *8 January 1986;*
Sunday *magazine, 18 March 1987*

Phil Collins met his wife **Jill** in a Los Angeles hotel bar. 'She hadn't a clue who I was, so I knew she wasn't talking to me because I was a pop star,' said Phil, whose first marriage ended in 1979 because of 'pressures of touring'.

From the Sun, *8 April 1986*

Lionel Ritchie met his wife **Brenda Harvey** while they were still at Tuskegee College, Alabama—but he had to persuade a friend to introduce them. She was only his second girlfriend, and he said: 'If I remember correctly, she was with one of her girlfriends at the time and I bought her a soda—but I was tongue-tied and just didn't know what to say to her. Thankfully finally I got up the nerve to ask her out.' He said later: 'The joke in my household is that the first girl who really paid attention to me and said "you could be someone wonderful", I married.'

From David Vaughan, 'Lionel Ritchie', *1984;* Daily Express, *18 March 1987*

Alannah Currie and **Tom Clarke** of the Thompson Twins met through a squat—and the former third member of the band, **Joe Leeway**. Alannah said: 'I'd met Joe at a party. He'd been going on about how he'd love to squat and I thought "yeah, you w**ker, I bet," and said there was a place going opposite mine.

'So he came down the next morning and I helped him break in but I think he was so scared on his own he only stayed for a couple of nights.'

Then Tom and another former band member moved in and Tom and Alannah met in the street. He subsequently used to go round to watch her all-girl group *The Unf***ables*.

'He'd come around in his old mac and sit against the wall,' said Alannah. 'He was just like a piece of the furniture. At one point, it was like letting the cat in.' But then when he took her to watch the original Thompson Twins perform, she became besotted. She joined the group 'to add a bit of madness'.

From Rosie Rouse, 'The Thompson Twins: An Odd Couple', *1985*

Jools Holland
Rock star, former presenter of 'The Tube'

Personal recipe for attracting the opposite sex
'I've not got a lot of time, let's step into this toilet.'

Ike and **Tina Turner** met after she jumped onstage while Ike was performing in St Louis and grabbed the mike. He didn't sign her up on the spot, but let her do some singing with his group at the Club Manhattan. Eventually love blossomed from their steamy performance at close working proximity.

From Ron Wynn, 'The Tina Turner Story',
1985

Dave Stewart and **Annie Lennox** of the Eurythmics met via a chain of coincidences sparked by a second-hand clothes stall at Camden Market. It all began when Paul Jacobs, who ran a record stall in the market, started dating Margo, the girl from the clothes stall, and through her met her 'music-mad' friend, Annie. Annie later moved into the flat above Paul's new shop in Crouch End, and one day Paul persuaded his friend Dave to come round to give Annie some advice on song contracts. The first words he said to me were, 'Will you marry me?' said Annie. 'I thought he was a serious nutter.'

From Johnny Waller and Steve Rapport,
'Eurythmics', 1986

Heroic Girls Who Made the First Move

Britt Ekland's first impression of one-time love **Rod Stewart** at Mick Jagger's birthday party was to pat him on the head, crush his spiky hair, and come up with the impressive line: 'Is this for real?' Later the two began their love affair cooing in a corner at a house party thrown by singing star **Cher**.

From Britt Ekland, 'True Britt', 1980

Julie Cool won her man, mad-cap impressionist **Phil**, at a party after he launched into a **Rolf Harris** impression. But he couldn't get his moustache off. He tells of her unusual chat-up technique: 'She took me into the kitchen and rubbed lard all over my face.'

From the Evening Standard, *22 December 1986*

Sheila Ferguson of the Three Degrees was lonely in 1978 because she said she and her two soul sisters were riding so high that no man would ask them for a date. But then in walked **Chris Robinson**, and Sheila slayed him with a great line in chat. 'Do you fool around?' she asked. 'Yes, can I have a kiss?' he replied. 'Not until we're engaged,' she said. So he took the ring off a Coca Cola can and plighted his troth. Three weeks later they married.

From the Daily Express, *8 April 1986*

Lizzie Webb
TV-am's fitness expert

Favourite chat-up line
'I've always been interested in "getting fit". Perhaps you could show me some exercises—privately?'
Worst chat-up line
'My diary is so full—I'll see if I've got a spare evening, I'd love to fit you in.' (Thus spoke a poser).

Another dusky beauty to get her man was Brazilian belle **Sylvia Martins**, who determined to get herself a slice of film star **Richard Gere** the moment her eyes fell on him at the cinema. Most girls might have given up there, but Sylvia managed to obtain his unlisted phone number. She purred down the line 'Hello, I'm Sylvia from Brazil.' He hung up. Most girls would definitely have given up there, but not our

Sylv. She adopted Plan B (the credit card company approach): find his favourite restaurant, and just hang in there, honey. He came in there. With a dazzling smile, she pounced. He being an officer and a gentleman (rather than just an American gigolo) just had to invite her to sit at his table. It was the start of an uplifting relationship.

From Woman's World, *February 1987*

Brigitte Neilsen became **Sylvester Stallone**'s girlfriend after bombarding him with letters. He said he tore them all up at first. Then he opened one which said how the flame-haired Danish model had been writing to him since she was eleven, when she first saw *Rocky*, and had always longed to meet him. He tore that one up too. Finally she played her ace: she sent him her modelling details. He said: 'I had always pictured her three feet tall and 400 pounds, with buck teeth and a horrendous complexion. But what I saw made me weak at the knees.' He rushed the two blocks to her hotel in the rain to find when he

---

Su Pollard
Star of BBC's 'Hi di Hi'

Favourite chat-up lines
'You should marry me, you know.'
'Excuse me, are you the sort of girl my mum told me to stay away from?'
'I may not look much, but I'm with the Woolwich.'
Worst chat-up lines
''Ello darlin'. You've been looking for me all your life.'
'Excuse me, have you got the time?'
'Nobody uses his brain like me. They're in me trousers.'
Best line tried on me
I got quite an amusing chat-up in a dreadful cocktail bar. This guy came up and said: 'What's a naff girl like you doing in a nice place like this?' Of course, I liked his cheek straight away and thus began a great relationship—I didn't marry him, though!

hammered at the door 'this wonderful vision'. He said: 'Well, I was only going to stay fifteen minutes, but I can stretch it to four hours.' Within weeks they were engaged.

From the Daily Star, *16 December 1985*

Cilla Black made a beeline for husband-manager **Bobby Willis** when he came into a Liverpool coffee bar sporting the richest of suntans. *Blind Date* presenter Cilla decided that he must be either foreign or rich, because no one in Liverpool had a suntan, and moved to introduce herself. He then sat down 'and spun a tale about going on a fabulous holiday working on a spaghetti plantation'. All very witty even if, yes, he did come from Liverpool.

From the Daily Star, *30 November 1985*

Lauren Hutton managed to land herself the (very rich) prince of the punk revolution, **Malcolm McLaren**, by boldly approaching a group of men in a Hollywood restaurant and demanding: 'Which one of you guys is Malcolm McLaren?' He told her he was the one and that she had crazy eyes. Said he later: 'She laughed. We had a drink at the bar, went on to a club and that was it.'

From the Daily Star, *28 March 1986*

Finally, **Grace Jones** hooked 6 foot 5½ inches Eurohunk **Dolph Lundgren** in Mae West style (not, as you might expect, with 'Let's forget about the 6 feet and talk about the 5½ inches,') when he gatecrashed a behind-the-scenes party in Sydney with a friend because they were hungry, and started troughing at the buffet laid on for the performers. Grace surrounded 'by all these drag queens and weirdos', according to Lundgren, stomped in, licked her lips and purred: 'What have we here, the main course?'

From Celebrity *magazine, November 1985*

Unusual Ways of Winning Friends and Influencing People Employed by Rock and Pop Stars

Dave Lee Roth, formerly of Van Halen, was a legend in the rock world because of his rather direct approach to a-wooing. This involved the assistance of several roadies equipped with walkie-talkie sets.

'That girl in the front row, red T-shirt—get rid of the boyfriend.' And when he was asked: 'What do you do when you get a girl back?', he replied 'I take off my clothes.'

It was Mr Lee Roth who convinced Lloyd's of London to insure him for £50,000 for legal costs arising from paternity suits. He had managed to convince the underwriters, with customary charm, that debauchery was 'instrumental' to his vocation.

'Do you ever get turned down by women?' he was asked by *Sounds*. 'I never ask,' he replied.

One interesting variation on the walkie-talkie routine came at a concert when he shouted out: 'I saw who threw that bottle and I'm gonna f*** your girlfriend.'

'You once said that every woman who wanted you would get you,' said *The Face*. 'Absolutely,' he replied. 'Do you want me? You only have to ask.'
From John Shearlaw, 'Van Halen, Jumping on the Dollar', 1984

Janis Joplin was another with a penchant for picking out her fans and fellow musicians, according to a biographer, issuing instructions to her roadies like 'I must have that bow-ah,' and 'He is *one* bee-yute-ee-full boy'.

To the subsequent reply: 'Why, he wouldn't even know what to do with you,' Janis drew herself up in a Mae West pose and drawled: 'What he doesn't know how to do, honey, I'll be glad to show him.'

She then apparently grabbed the bow-ah (a blond bass player) and held him in a ferocious arm-lock. 'You're not climbing on

Alan Robson
Commercial radio DJ

Favourite chat-up lines
'I've sprained my wrists carrying an injured child. Could you help me to unbutton my boxer shorts?'

'It's hot in here, let's go somewhere and loosen our clothes before we pass out.'

'Do you fancy a drive? I've got an HGV outside—a Heavy Groping Vehicle.'

'Let's get involved in some lip-lock, it's the world championship next week.'

Worst chat-up lines
'Sex appeal—give generously.'

'Has anyone told you, you've got beautiful . . .'

Personal recipe for attracting the opposite sex
I'm a great believer in going with the flow. My show deals with love problems and it seems that men are very attracted to women who show themselves to be attracted to them.

1 Be interested, sparkle with fun, and wave £1,000 in loose bills around.

2 Mention loudly 'I've just had my Aids screening and I'm clear'.

3 Women are attracted to complete bastards—we good guys don't get half the chances the bad 'uns have— so I'm a little bad at weekends.

4 Learn to breathe through your ears and kiss like Dyno-Rod at full power.

5 Get a job where you work 9 to 5 instead of 10.00 at night until 2.00 like me.

a bus going somewhere tonight, are you honey?' No you're not, man, they told me you were going to a party, man. 'I thought we'd go back to the dressing room and get it on.'

From 'Janis Joplin: A Piece of my Heart',
1986

Ozzy Osbourne's zany bat-eating lifestyle apparently makes use of his reputation for the occult. The former Black Sabbath star has told how his repertoire extends to winning the women with practical jokes. Thus after renting an apartment in Los Angeles and sitting around for much of the day, he had become familiar with an automatic gas fire in one of the rooms which would sporadically emit a jet of flame from the grate. 'I got to the point that I knew exactly when it was about to happen, down to the very second. So what I used to do, whenever there was a new chick over, I would start ranting on at her, telling her that all that stuff about black magic and me was *true*. And just as she was on the edge of believing what I was telling her, I'd suddenly stick my arms out in the air and puff! Big jet of flame shoots out of the wall, and the fire comes on! If they managed to survive that without a heart attack, I'd let them hang around for a while.'

From Mick Wall, 'Ozzy Osbourne: Diary of a
Madman', 1984

Finally, **Julio Iglesias** used an unusual approach when confronted by **Marina Ripa Mena**, the wife of **Count Carlo**, Italian EEC commissioner, and nicknamed 'The Naked Duchess'. According to her book, *My First 40 Years*—a bestseller in Italy—he laid his hands on her legs and cooed: 'What a tasty piece of ham.'

From the Daily Mirror, *13 December 1984*

9

Love Letters and Poems

Make no mistake, the modern sophisticate can learn much from the tactics of his forebears, especially when 'getting it on' (or off) might have taken some months or even years. Today's romantic message is more likely to be a curt postcard to Radio 1 saying: 'Tell Gail we'll all get together and have a big night out and canyerplay'er *I Should Be So Lucky*. In the days of yore, it was different. 'More than kisses, letters mingle souls,' wrote John Donne: see if you're up to matching any of these:

'Oh if I were there I could put my arms so close about your neck, hush you into softest sleep . . . Goodnight, my beloved, dream of me.'

Jayne to Thomas Carlyle

'My dearest, beloved Emma, the dear friend of my bosom, I have no thought except you and that French Fleet.'

Nelson to Lady Hamilton

'I hope before long to crush you in my arms and cover you with a million kisses.'

Napoleon to Josephine

'You are all things to me . . . I can see nothing beyond you.'

Elizabeth Barrett Browning

'You have ravished me away by a power I cannot resist . . . I cannot breathe without you.'

John Keats

'I'd sell my toes to see you.'

Dylan Thomas

Chat-up Line

Debrett's Modern Manners gives some interesting pointers in 'opening gambits' for social encounters. The idea, says the tome loftily, is 'to discover what interests your neighbour has and to do so with as few daft questions as possible.' One experienced dinner guest is praised for asking as an opener: 'What is the nicest thing that has happened to you today?' The shy are advised to make a mental list of possible subjects, which, say the authors, should be topical, neutral, and certainly not about politics. Possible suggestions are:

● 'What a cold December we are having. If you weren't in England where would you like to be at this time of year?'
● 'I hear you are off to Greece for three weeks. What books are you packing in your suitcase?'

● 'What beautiful flowers Anne (the hostess) always has—do you like gardening?'
● 'If you were the Queen, what opera/ ballet/play would you choose to have performed for your Gala?'
● 'Are you a Wimbledon fan? Have you been watching it?'
● 'What delicious claret—are you a connoisseur of wine?'

This has given the neighbour a chance to say if he is interested in travel, art, literature, sport, music, gardening, food . . . let us hope he will have responded favourably to a bait.

From Elsie Burch Donald (ed), 'Debrett's Etiquette and Modern Manners', *1981*

'A wanton tongue—yet chaste and holy, stole between my lips! What were you doing? You were secretly kissing me.'

Charles Kingsley to Fanny Grenfell

'Woe to you, my princess, when I come. I will kiss you quite red and feed you until you are plump. And if you are forward you shall see who is the stronger, a gentle little girl who doesn't eat or a big wild man who has cocaine in his body.'

Sigmund Freud to Martha Bernays

Perhaps romantic letter writing at its best could be read flowing from the florid, seventeenth-century pen of George Villiers, second Duke of Buckingham. He was the master of the compliment:

'Her face is so smooth that the eye slides off it—smooth as Waller's verse—smooth as the path of day that's beat in Heaven by the swift wheels of the ever-travelling sun.'

And his unsurpassable writing in the second person:

'I desire all, hope little, and dare ask nothing. It would content me if you did but dream of me, or if I could dream that you did so, but I shall never sleep enough for thinking of you to dream at all. If you allow me only your face and outward dress, I am no more beholding to you than you are to your looking-glass. You are in everything a goddess, but that you will not be moved by prayers.'

From John Harold Wilson, 'A Rake and His Times', 1954

Love letters nevertheless have sometimes had their dubious side. Henry VIII wrote to Anne Boleyn: 'I promise to take you as my sole mistress, casting off all others than yourself.'

Sometimes if not burned they only lead to tears, of course. Long before 'Bunnies Can and Will Go to France', Oscar Wilde was in trouble for an affectionate epistle to young Lord Alfred Douglas: 'My Own Boy, Your sonnet is quite lovely, and it is a marvel that those red rose-leaf lips of yours should have been made no less for music of song than for madness of kisses.'

Another risky one, from foot-fetishist Fedor Dostoevsky to his wife to be, Anna Snitkina: 'I go down on my knees before you and I kiss your dear feet countless number of times. I imagine this every minute and I enjoy it . . . I bear witness that I long to kiss every toe on your foot and you will see I shall achieve my purpose.'

Perhaps the most astonishing love letters written of old were by James Joyce to his wife to be, Nora Barnacle. Mr Joyce alternated between the poetic: 'My beautiful wild flower of the hedges! My dark-blue rain-drenched flower!'

. . . and the plainly erotic: 'I would be delighted to feel my flesh tingling under your hand . . . to feel your hot lecherous lips . . . My darling little convent girl. There is some star too near the earth for I am still in a fever-fit of animal desire.'

Sheer Poetry

You need to know 'Let's Do It' by Cole Porter:

'And that's why
Birds do it, bees do it,
Even educated fleas do it.

Let's do it,
Let's fall in love.'

'A Subaltern's Love Song' by John Betjeman:
'Miss J. Hunter Dunn, Miss J. Hunter Dunn,
Furnish'd and burnish'd by Aldershot sun,
What strenuous singles we played after tea,
We in a tournament—you against me!'

And 'Celia Celia' by Adrian Mitchell:
'When I am sad and weary,
When I think all hope has gone,
When I walk along High Holborn
I think of you with nothing on.'

Apart from that, you might try the odd undiscovered gem. Like this from Marcus Argentarius, 1st Century BC/AD, entitled 'Lysidice':
'Take off those flimsy nets, Lysidice;
Don't twitch your bottom teasingly at me,
Walking about in your transparent dress
Although it suits you well, I must confess;
The muslin clings so tightly to your sides
It shows more of your body than it hides.'

10

Natural Romantic Situations and How to Make the Most of Them

Outside satanic orgies, church socials, Harrods' sales and bus queue punch-ups, there are, of course, certain natural situations where opposite sexes are literally thrown together. The secret of 'pulling' power is how to, naturally, make the best of these fleeting moments of heady opportunity.

On Public Transport

This is a boon for men, because of all those up-jumped fellows who think they've really made it when they get their first firm's car. The ratio is down for a start. When you think of it, there is little more accidental physical contact you will get in your life than a crowded bus, train or tube. And think of all you've got in common: the weather, the late trains, a hangover. Make the most of it!

Ploys: Never sit down straight away. Look around for likely targets and sit next to them. (Think about it. If you try to sit on your own you're always troubled by a load of half-wits. Why not choose your company?).

Carry a provocative book, e.g. *The Sex Life of the Eskimo*, *101 Ways to Make Love on the Tube*. Suddenly fall on top of your target, apologizing profusely, 'I can never get the hang of these handrails/straps.'

If you really want to be popular, grab the conductor's ticket punch, then make off down the train shouting: 'British Rail is pleased to announce that today every second-class passenger can travel first for free.'

Chat-up Line

The New York Road Runners Club were swift in 1986 to end that most poignant of laments: the loneliness of the long distance runner. *New York Running News* came up with the idea of a 'lonely feet column' for its 25,000 readers and soon afterwards reported that, in a very solitary sport, couples, were, yes, getting it together. At a dollar a word, it also made the club money, of course. 'We've heard that they are very satisfied with the responses,' said Raleigh Mayer, editor of the magazine, according to her own ad as a market test: 'a tough cookie, 26, ready to crumble for an uncompromising character male.' In a world dominated 2:1 by men (the reverse of the general New York predator-woman-dominated dating market) it was of course an ideal new way for girls to meet middle-class, well-educated, high income males. But there was an Achilles heel, of course. One 'Travelling marathoner of a certain age' who told 'before responding, beware—running is my world' got no replies at all. He was Fred Lebow, president of the Road Runners Club.

From the Daily Mail, *9 September 1986*

EXAMPLES

Is this the 8.02 or last night's 20.52 running late?

Do you mind if I lean across and open the window (and make a meal of it!)?

It's amazing to see someone up so early and looking so vibrant.

I could sit on your knee, but I think it would make the other passengers jealous.

Is being late on trains a hobby of yours?

Would you like to elbow me in the ribs now
in case I accidentally nudge you?
Let me ring the bell for you.
Let me have a laugh. Let me see the photo
in your bus pass.
Well, I had to hold on to *something*.

On an Air Journey

Beware here! Stewardesses (and stewards)
have had more practice at fending off the
determined among you than any other pro-
fession. They are used to staying in the best
hotels, mingling with pop stars, international
jet setters, and a bit of rough stuff for light
relief as well. So homework is essential. Otherwise, stick to your fellow passengers.

Ploys: Struggle with your luggage. Someone
is bound to help. If you don't like the look of
them, feign Popeye and suggest you've just
digested half a ton of spinach.

On the plane, jacknife out your foot at the
strategic moment. If you time it right, your
target is bound to fall into your lap (make sure
they're not carrying a pot of coffee or a sick bag
though.)

After take-off stand up and shout accusingly:
'I have reason to believe one of you has not
read the safety leaflet.' If you really want to
make an impression, go right to the front of the
cabin, grab the loudspeaker handset and
announce: 'The drinks are on the Captain!'

EXAMPLES
To a fellow passenger:
Have you seen the airline loo scene in *Rich
and Famous*?
I think they're a bit short, do you mind if I
share your blanket?
Do you know why these pilots do all this
Delta, Charlie and Rogering?
Him to Stewardess:
Do you do much travelling in your job?
I can get you a membership form for the
mile-high club.
I just love a girl half in uniform.
If I said I was free, would you do your duty?
Her to the pilot:
Are your flaps up or down right now?
What do you have to do to get one of those
armbands?

Do you talk like that at night? You know,
'this is your Captain speaking'?
Who's the best between the sheets, you or
your automatic pilot?

At the Supermarket

Where else could you meet so many hungry
young women/men? Apart from the obvious,
like ramming targets with a trolley or very
deliberately setting up a very sensual
avocado-tweaking session with half the shop,
'I'm sure it isn't ripe, go on, feel,' there is
everyone's inner soul laid bare right there in
those all-revealing chariots of wire.

Ploys: On the top of your shopping, place
pathetic portions for one, to evoke pangs of
sympathy among your fellow shoppers.

Stand by the fridge, casually open a pack of
processed cheese and ask your target to take a
test bite. If she's hesitant, tell her it's being
filmed for a TV advert and on screen you'll be
swapped for Leslie Crowther.

Shout (very loudly) 'I've been raped! Fetch
the store detective' (especially effective for
men). Then faint. Explain later as they all
rush to take you home that it was just one of
your turns.

EXAMPLES

Would you like to ride on my trolley?

You look a bit of a brand leader yourself.

Race you to the checkout.

Wouldn't you think they'd fit these things
with rubber bumpers?

Funny . . . I never knew trout smoked.

If I were to invite you round for dinner, would
you like Heinz or own-brand beans on your
toast?

You have the sexiest way of tweaking a lemon.

Can you tell me if this is the oil they anoint
each other with at Hollywood parties?

(Pointing at security cameras) I wonder what
they up there are thinking about us down
here?

My uncle once ran Harrods. But the store
detective still caught him.

Chat-up Facts

In 1985 Professor Thomas Murray, head of English language at a university in Ohio, logged 500 hours in 50 singles bars in and around St Louis, Missouri, to compose the first ever chart of chat-up lines for the journal *America Speech*. The approaches, he said, could be divided into three categories:

Compliments ('The mark of the desperate wimps,' observed the professor): These were led by 'Best knockers I've seen all night' and 'What skilful-looking hands'.

Questions: 'What's your name?' he found used 156 times, but 53 asked straight out 'Wanna f. . . ?' and, in all, 377 'used variations on this theme'. ('Wanna make it?' 'Wanna do it?' 'Wanna saddle up?')

Advertisements: Both sexes preferred 'My name is' (110 times) but used 'I want you' 59 times. Regular male 'ads' were 'I love cherries', 'I'm a retread' (meaning divorced), and for some reason 'I'm a cannibal.'

Popular female uses of this approach were: 'I want to play', 'My ears are warm', 'My can is empty', 'I love lollipops' and 'My bunny really hops'.

Some of the chat-up questions are merely abbreviations: BC? 'Birth Control?' MQ? 'Meaningful Quickie?' and MOY? 'My place or yours?'

Naughtier male chat-up lines were: 'Wanna tinker with my toy?' (1) and 'Wanna honk my horn?' (5). But the women were apparently more daring with 'Is Willie home?' (37); 'Can Willie come out to play?' (31); 'Like art?' (9) and 'Can I doddle your doodle?' (2).

On the Beach

What could be a more natural aphrodisiac than sand, sea and Sangria? There is something about the atmosphere of a beach—all those stripped sun-tanned bodies, the fact you're so far away from reality—that puts everyone in the mood for love. It's up to you to exploit it.

Ploys: Play patience or do a jigsaw on the end of your towel. Someone is bound to come along and kick the whole thing all over the beach.

Wear a T-shirt with a provocative message, like 'Shall I take it off and the lower half too?' or 'Anyone want to swop this T-shirt for a can of Fosters?'

Offer to rub sun cream on your target's back, but substitute Raljex.

EXAMPLES

Do you mind me asking how many times you turn an hour?

Would your boyfriend/girlfriend mind if I kicked sand in his/her face?

How would you like to put your toes on the end of my mat?

I'll write a book for you. I'll call it 'Beauty and the Beach'.

The beach can be very bad for jellyfish. Let me take you by the hand.

Is shingle your favourite type of beach or do you prefer concrete?

You could be the best fun I've had without playing frisbee.

How would you like to sail out to sea in a beautiful pea-green boat?

Him to her:

You've heard of a lounge lizard? Well I'm a sand lizard.

Her to him:

I hope you don't mind me telling you, but you've got your shorts on inside out.

Simon Williams
Stage, TV and film actor

Favourite chat-up lines
Girl in disco: 'I suppose you think you look like Simon Williams.'
Simon Williams: 'Er. Yes. Sometimes.'
Girl in disco: 'Never mind. Dance.'

Personal recipe for attracting the opposite sex
I've never discovered the secret of the simultaneous need to be red hot and icy cool.

At the Discotheque

The traditional venue for meeting the opposite sex is rather blemished by being (1) noisy, so the onus is on to look good rather than sound good; (2) competitive; and (3) keeping hours not very compatible with getting up at 6.50 in the morning for work.

However, if you've got the get and go to get up and go (and take heed of the advice in this book), you're sure to come out tops.

Ploys: Buy a drink, find someone you like, bump right into them, spill the lot, and make them buy another.

For extra attention, shout to the DJ 'come out of that box up there—we all know you're only 4′ 2″.'

Tell the bouncer your target has just groped you and is on his way to grope the barmaid/ barman. Then collect your coat, rush outside and stand with hand outstretched to catch them when they're thrown out, hopefully before they crash headfirst into the pavement.

EXAMPLES
Would you carry my books back from the disco?
We have obviously entered a music-free zone.
Are you deaf, or do your feet automatically tap the opposite beat to the music?

Who welded you to the dance floor? My friend could lend you an oxyacetylene torch.
There are lots of teethmarks in your earlobes.
You should be at the Hippodrome with feet like that.
If music be the food of love, do you think the DJ's got appendicitis?
Him to her:
Hold still, there's a tarantula on your eyelids.
Do you have a licence for those stilettos?
What did you use to paint your nails, gloss or distemper?

At the Launderette

Nick Kamen made it famous, of course. It's a dismal sort of venue, but where else to meet single young people in need of a helping hand and captive for a couple of hours for you to weave your magic? As well as the shared rather basic experience, there is the added intimacy of baring all, i.e. where else outside the bedroom would you clock what sort of undies he/she wears?

Ploys: Sit there reading *Playboy/Playgirl*. It's a conversation piece.
Strip to your undies, climb in the dryer (and quickly out again), proclaiming: 'That's better, I just had to get warm.'
Take a pair of scanty briefs belonging to the opposite sex, then at a strategic moment hold them aloft, saying: 'Are these yours?'
Walk in on another night with just a pair of socks/stockings and announce at the door: 'This is all I've got this week. Is anybody prepared to put them in with their load?'

EXAMPLES

I bet if you and I got our act together, we could really clean up.
See the moths have been at your Levis too.
How would you like to contribute to my favourite charity—Rinse Aid?
What's your favourite soap?
Hmm—no pyjamas. So you obviously sleep in the nude. . . .
Don't worry, it'll be all white on the night.
I bet you're only here to get your brain boil-washed.

We could make a film—you beautiful, this my launderette.

Her to him:

That's the largest pair of underpants I ever saw.

You don't look an Omo type to me.

Gillian Taylforth
Star of BBC TV's 'Eastenders'

Favourite chat-up lines

'Why don't you come round for breakfast . . . tonight!'

'You can put your slippers under my bed anytime!'

'You can share my toast in the morning.'

Worst chat-up lines

'I'd like to show you my etchings!'

'What's a nice girl like you doing in a place like this?'

Personal recipe for attracting the opposite sex

Trying to look as if I'm interested!

Him to her:

Hmm. New improved Comfort—that's ma' favourite per-foom.

At the Office

Well, you spend most of the day working there so why not make the office work for you? The golden rules are (1) never anyone on the same floor (somebody else may already be doing it on the same floor); no, seriously, and (2) never, *never* with your secretary or boss (especially if you're both the same sex.)

Ploys: Let it be known you have a complete list of computer passwords. Everyone forgets theirs, it's a fact, and they will flock to you.

If you don't have a computer, get a master key for everyone's desks—they'll always lock themselves out.

If you see your target going to the coffee machine, go there too and spill your Gold Blend all over them. Hang by the lift until someone interesting appears. Dive in there with them, then throw all the switches and feign a fainting fit.

EXAMPLES

Hi! I'm new here and I've just come to match up the faces to the internal phone book.

How would you like to join me in the staff canteen? We could get indigestion together.

What are you doing during the rush hour?

There is nothing I wouldn't do for a new desk/office/executive ashtray, etc.

I'll trade my desk-top calculator for your executive intrusion facility trimphone.

Can you take a hint without me having to spill coffee all over you?

Why don't we pretend this afternoon that it's the office Christmas party?

If we went to the office cupboard, would you remain stationary?

At the Library

Cosy, sedate and full of intelligent people, where could be better for starting a relationship? The problem is, I suppose, that anyone there, from librarians through struggling authors to the poor unemployed, won't have a bean between them. But no matter.

Ploys: Ask the assistant to reach to the highest shelf. They will get a little ladder and feel completely uncomfortable about this, which gives you a chance to lend a hand.

Stand deliberately in the middle of the library reading room and shout, at the very top of your voice: 'You boring old boots, why are you all so quiet in here?' Again, a lot of people will have something to say to you after that.

EXAMPLES

Have you got the latest Charles Dickens?

Which way for the dirty books, please?

Did you read her last one? ('No, neither did I.')

If you give me a Pound, I'll lend you my T. S. Eliot.

Let me tell you who the murderer was, and save you the trouble.

Excuse me groping on the floor, but my microfilm's just run off under your desk. Can you tell me how I go about reserving a librarian?

Sue Robbie
Presenter of ITV's 'Connections'

Favourite chat-up lines
I can never remember them because at the time they seem utterly convincing and unplanned!

Worst chat-up lines
'If I ever see your double I will make a point of going out with it.' It! (In a fan letter received March 1987).
'Please go out with me. You don't have to say yes. I'll understand. I *will* start going to discos and I'll try to be less boring.' (In a letter to a 13-year-old friend of mine received February 1987).

At the Health/Sports Club

Well, what could be better for attracting the opposite sex than a healthy body. And men, it's definitely the place for the best-looking girls. The problem is, of course, that health and sports clubs naturally encourage the height of competition, and you might have to put up with a few aches and pains, not to mention thrashings on the courts, to achieve your goal.

Ploys: Always take a broken piece of equipment, e.g. broken badminton racket, shoe missing a lace, etc. so you can do the rounds looking for someone suitable to borrow from. Then you'll owe them something and can be forever offering!

Among your designer gear, wear some outrageous extraneous equipment, e.g. goggles. They'll think it's the latest sports fashion and all try to copy it next week.

To be truly tantalizing and break down their resistance, stroll into the club bar carrying a book on desserts, e.g. '*101 Recipes for Chocolate Cake*'.

EXAMPLES

If I let you win at tennis, would you jump over the net and kiss me?

If I come to the cricket match, would you let me score?

Jogging:

Do you fancy a quick detour to compare our speeds/heartbeat/body temperatures?

Athletics:

When we reach the wall, can you give me a leg up, please?

When you're not vaulting, what do you do with your pole?

Golf:

What's your handicap, apart that is from your looks?

How's your foreplay?

On the tennis court:

Singles or doubles?

I could give you a good volley.

Him to her:

I've done a lot of practice on my forehand.

I think you'll like my service.

Do you think I'll ever get beyond the baseline?

Her to him:

Do you play with new or old balls?

11

Advice from the Sexperts

So what do the professionals in the business of oiling the wheels of the caravan of love— and those most involved—suggest?

How to Win Your Man

One of the first 'candid' books to tell a girl really what's what was of course *Sex and the Single Girl* by **Helen Gurley Brown**. 'You get to a man by dealing with him at his professional level,' she later summed up. 'Then stay around to charm and sexually zonk him.' The message: if you see a likely fish in the sea, then make sure a friend introduces you, and if he is a millionaire, trip him up.

Cynthia Hempel suggests a methodical, battle-plan approach to a 'vision' of a man

you might see across a crowded room. You must not march up to him and say 'wanna get high?' or try and floor him with a flying tackle.

Instead you must (1) watch him covertly for a while, giving him the occasional 'come hither' look; (2) go and stand next to him 'a little bit more closely than you think you should'; and (3) shut up (for the time being)!

'He will become intensely aware of you and slightly nervous. This is where you say something casually intimate, as if you've known him for years. Something along the lines of 'Do you think that man in the green suit is wearing a corset?' Or 'This is the first time I've worn this dress, and I'm still not sure I like the bow-on-the-shoulder effect. What are your thoughts?'

Liz Hobbs
World international water-skiing champion

Favourite chat-up lines

'Excuse me, do you mind if I fall in love with you?'

'Can I cook you breakfast?'

(*I was judging a beauty contest*): 'You've got the most sensational legs I've ever seen, would you mind if I looked at the top to see if they go right up to your bum?'

Worst chat-up lines

'Haven't I seen you somewhere before?' ('No, and you probably won't again!').

'Have you got a light?' ('No, I don't smoke and how can you imagine a woman would be attracted to snogging an ashtray?').

'What's a nice girl like you doing in a place like this?' ('I thought I'd like to see how the rough end of town had fun—tell me!').

Best lines tried on me

The worst ones are more frequent. If people know who you are they automatically assume you want to talk about your sport—when you're having fun, you don't. A chat-up line including my sport automatically puts up a barrier for me.

Personal recipe for attracting the opposite sex

Nice guys seem to like the pretty, shy reserved attitude and look. A glance in the right direction at the right time usually does the trick!

'Then he'll say something, then you'll say something, then there you'll be making a date for the movies next Thursday.'

From Cynthia Hempel, 'Sex Tips for Girls', 1984

Cosmopolitan columnist **Tom Crabtree** also recommends the direct approach: 'Men aren't all that good at communication and fear dreadfully for their masculinity. To be too subtle with men is like reading Donne's poetry to a basking seal. I can't for the life of me think why you can't phone up a man you fancy and say, 'I'm K. We met at Y.' (Describe yourself. You're allowed to exaggerate.) Then ask him to the theatre/concert/cinema. He might say no. He could well say yes. Simpler still, invite him to tea and tell him you bake a very mean chocolate cake. I've never met a man yet who wasn't mad for chocolate cake.'

From Cosmopolitan, *August 1984*

Wendy Stehling came up in 1985 with a rather aggressive book called *How to Find a Husband in 30 Days*. The advice could be summarized as 'go geddem', advising cruising the car showrooms looking for men looking at posh cars or turning up at the car wash ('men keep saying how they love to hold the big, heavy hose').

New York Daily News writer **Rosemary Breslin** actually tried it. She said: 'The first guy was really cute: we met at a night club. I wore a skirt as Stehling advised. So did he. His was nicer with a trendy black on black print. It's fashionable for men to wear skirts these days so don't get the wrong idea, but it's hard when his legs are better than yours. If it all works out, the wedding could be interesting. Who will wear the wedding gown? Will my father attend?'

And the supermarket trolley? Miss Breslin managed to ram the same man twice. It wasn't a recipe for love. 'He threatened to floor me if it happened again,' she reported.

From Wendy Stehling, 'How to Find a Husband in 30 Days', 1985; Daily Star, *10 September 1985;* Daily Mail, *18 June 1985*

How to Win Your Girl

The author's favourite advice comes in a book called *The Art of Erotic Seduction* by Dr **Albert Ellis** and **Roger O. Conway**: 'Help women when they are carrying heavy objects. This includes assisting strange women you may run into—and whom you may thereby be able to pick up. Learn the art of listening. Give them half a chance to tell you every foolish little thing that has happened to them since you soul-kissed last Sunday and before they realize what has struck them, you may be on your way.'

It would be worthwhile mentioning to the chaps this sage warning from one of the old-time favourites, **Dorothy Dix** (*Her Book, Funk and Wagnalls*, New York, 1926), whose words are probably even more valid today. The main thing is to choose the right time to pounce:

'Never pop the question to the business girl in the morning of a sunshiny day when she has on a new frock and a good hat and everything is going swimmingly at the office and she feels fit and fine and ready to buck the world. Instead, choose a rainy evening, when she is sitting alone at home, dejected and forlorn, when she is tired and the boss has been grumpy. Then the thing she wants most on earth is just a nice, strong masculine shoulder to cry on.'

The world's leading gigolo, sixty-three-year-old **Giovanni Rovai**, travelled to Britain in October 1984 to tell the magic of how he had managed to seduce some 3,000 women.

First rule: never touch alcohol. Yes, for liquor is too powerful and confuses the brain. What you have to do is to use your mind. 'You must give your all,' said Giovanni.

So the steps to seduction? It's all to do with touch:
Step 1, touch her with your eyes 'to undermine her resistance';

Step 2, kiss her shoulders;
Step 3, kiss her neck; and
Step 4, seize the opportunity before it is
past—you must kiss her feet!
  Yes, that's where we've all been going
wrong!

One interesting survivor's guide which came
to my attention was *A Witch's Guide to Love
and Lust* by Miss **Jean Williams** (*quoted in the*
News of the World, *22 May 1983*) which says
that to win the girl you only need to touch
her and whisper the magic words:
  'Touch of lust
  Turn to me
  Your body to mine
  Your lust to me
  Make you mine.'

And who can forget the advice of the
monogamous world's most married man,
Glyn 'Scottie' Wolfe of Blythe, California.
'Women are easy. I keep a large bottle of
whisky in the house. A large Scotch is the
best pants-remover I know of.'

John Kettley
BBC TV weatherman

Favourite chat-up lines
Certainly a conversation about the
weather would be a 'dry' subject. One
of my own lines, which raises a titter,
is: 'How about a drink back at my
place? I've got my own ISOBAR.

  One weather person to another
might say 'Come back to my place and
let me work on your "baroclinic
zones".' (Cf 'erogenous zones').

Worst chat-up line
'How about a warm front and a cold
front getting together and raising the
pressure?'

Personal recipe for attracting the opposite sex
Keep off the garlic.
I met my wife in a pub and our eyes
met over an onion sandwich—she
hates onions and I was feeling hungry.

You have heard from the sexperts. But what about our favourites of stage and screen? **Patrick Duffy** of *Dallas* is obviously a medallion man at heart, putting it all down to flashy attire.

'A woman has to be dressed to kill. Plunging neckline, slit skirt, very high heels and lots of jewellery. Her dress material should be so sheer and clingy that underwear is out of the question. The right clothes for a man are casual—but smart. The shirt should be open to the waist, with a hairy chest and lots of gold chains showing. A deep suntan would be a great help too. It doesn't really matter what you say to each other, so long as you look right.'

From the Daily Star, *2 April 1985*

Flirting Hints for the Guys

Doug Sanders, international golfer, recommended among other things:
● Touch. Latin-American and Mediterranean peoples use their hands freely to express warmth. Frequently touching a woman—on her hands and arms, on her face and neck, on her back, on her knees—sets up a feeling of real intimacy. As the ad for Yellow Pages: let your fingers do the walking.
● Talk right and don't be a phoney. Direct your conversation to things concerning a woman, not yourself. Talk about sex. Don't make it sound dirty, please. A few questions or comments like: 'You have pretty lips', or 'I bet you're a good kisser', or 'Are you warm?' can get your relationship on to an intimate plane right away. If she hits you or goes running from the room it means your nostrils started to flare and your tongue came out. Go back and practise conversation with the dog.

*From Doug Sanders' autobiography, '*Come Swing With Me*', 1974*

Joan Collins, *Dynasty* star, says a man who can make her laugh has the best chance of winning her heart:
'I just base everything on the premise that

all men are basically seven-year-olds. 'That sounds cynical, but it isn't really. I do think men are much more like little boys than women are like little girls.'

From the Sun, *13 January 1985*

Wincey Willis
TV-am's weather presenter

Favourite chat-up line
There really aren't any good lines—sincerity is what counts.

Worst chat-up line
'Hey Wincey, is that where you keep your ferrets?'

But **Lesley Anne Jones**, showbusiness journalist, believes that today with wit extending little further than 'It's yer lucky day', 'Get 'em off' and 'Your place or mine?', the verbal side of romance is dead. 'Far more subtle is my hot-blooded banker friend who often says he's going away for a week or two and offers to lend his apartment. Then he says: "But you'll have to come back with me so I can show you how the gadgets work." '

From the Sun, *25 January 1985*

Julio Iglesias, international crooner, believes closeness is the key: 'I like to hold a woman's eyes with my own. I never let my eyes leave her, because for every moment I am with her, I am giving her my full attention. To me, there is no one else in the world who is more important. When I talk to her, I whisper so that she has to bend her ear close to my mouth. When I walk with her, I hold her arm. Touch is so important to women. I always make the first move. That way, she feels she has control of the situation and can pull back if she wishes.'

From the Daily Star, *2 April 1985*

Mike Nolan, Bucks Fizz star, says the right move is to pose a challenge to a girl. 'Sometimes I ask two girls whether they'd like a nice cosy threesome with me, and because I get straight to the point, they usually agree.'

From the Sun, *19 September 1983*

Flirting Hints for the Girls

Linda Evans, *Dynasty* star, says that flirting is the gentle, teasing way to make romantic music together: 'I start out with eye contact across a crowded room. You know, the sort of thing where you hold the other person's gaze for just a second or two longer than is necessary. Then I look away and pretend to be deeply in conversation. I'll wait fully ten minutes before I stare again—and I make sure he catches me doing it! That's the moment to allow a little half-smile.'

From the Daily Star, *2 April 1985*

Britt Ekland has this advice to get your man: 'If you find yourself a temporary wallflower you will look more approachable if you sip slowly on a drink. If you are left literally twiddling your thumbs, you must *not* fidget. Just as slow movements are infinitely more sensuous, so is leisurely speech. If you want to get cosy with someone, try sitting curled up in a semi-fetal position, which looks very feminine.'

From Britt Ekland, 'Sensual Beauty and How to Achieve It', *1983*

Suzanne Dando, TV actress: 'Men like my hair up and the gap in my teeth. They are always telling me this. When you meet a man you want to make him feel special. Share a plate of food with him at a party and be fun. Show him you've got lots of personality.'

From the Sunday Mirror, *16 December 1984*

Linda Ronstadt, American singing star: 'My theory has always been that if something doesn't smell right you should never fight it. But if it does smell right it's a way of gene codes signalling to each other that it would be a good genetic combination. That's why you can be attracted to people

Sally Jones

BBC Breakfast Time and Britain's first woman sportscaster

Favourite chat-up lines (and the best tried on me)

'Hello, you've got the most marvellous bottom. Would you consider appearing as a nude back view in a play I'm putting on in Oxford?'

'Hello, I saw you in the Bodleian Library today and I bribed the librarian to tell me your name and college. Will you come to *Measure for Measure* with me at Stratford in a few minutes? I've got the tickets and a car waiting outside.'

Worst chat-up lines

'Hi, my name's Robert Blumerfeld. Back home in Georgia my father's got a walk-in humidor for his cigars . . .'

On a first (and last) date: 'I've just got back after working in the Sudan—and I had an Aids test—which was negative. Have you had an Aids test yet?'

While interviewing Dave Allen: 'Ooh, you're nice. They usually send some awful sweaty man with BO to interview me.'

Personal recipe for attracting the opposite sex

Never accept the first offer of a date. Don't let your eyes wander over their shoulder at parties.
Tease them unmercifully.

that you don't like very much—because they have the right breeding.'
From the Daily Mirror, *27 September 1985*

Finally, **Heidi Abromowitz**, erstwhile alter ego of American comedienne **Joan Rivers**, has these tips on how to 'undress for success':

Never let a knicker line show around your ankles.

Never wear anything that leaves something to the imagination.
Never wear anything made of rubber.
Always wear flame retardant tights.
Always wear leather.
Always remember that wearing less will get you more.
Always wear your partner out first.
From Joan Rivers, 'The Life and Times of Heidi Abromowitz', 1984

12

Where Celebrities Get it Together

Any keen celebrity-watcher will observe that, just as for the more humdrum rest of us, most people meet at work, i.e. on the stage or set. But by no means all . . .

Stars for Whom it All Began on the Set

Andrew Lloyd Webber and **Sarah Brightman** met when she auditioned for his show *Cats*. She said: 'I remember thinking what a nice man, but nothing more. I got the job, but there was no immediate flame there.' It was at a party after the musical *Nightingale* when he went up to her and said: 'I just didn't know you could sing like that; I didn't know about your voice.' A fairytale romance was born.

From the Daily Express, *1 April 1985*

The Krankies—husband and wife team Ian and Janette Tough—met as teenagers making their debut at the Pavilion Theatre, Glasgow. Janette was a 'babe' in pantomime and Ian was apprenticed as a theatre electrician. She caught his eye and he would sit in the lighting gallery high above the stage and throw toffees to her.

Little was young Romeo to know but she actually hated toffees, and used to tuck them into her knickers to give away later. However, by the end of the pantomime season they had formed a professional and personal partnership. Two years later they were married.

One man who met two loves of his life on the set was **Sting** of Police—first, in a

Leslie Crowther
Leading TV presenter. Compère of 'The Price is Right'

Worst chat-up lines
Any that have been delivered by me! I used to recite 'Shall I compare thee to a Summer's day?' (Shakespeare sonnet) to any of the girls I could lure into the bushes at the Open Air Theatre, Regent's Park in 1949— mind you, I was only 16 so it didn't have much effect!

Personal recipe for attracting the opposite sex
No recipe needed when you're on a diet! Mind you, one can still look at the menu.

Christmas show in 1974, he met Irish actress **Frances Tomelty**. Second, **Trudie Styler**, whom he met when she appeared down the

bill to his then wife in a production of *Macbeth*.

From Mick St Michael, 'Backstage: Accompanying the Police', 1985

Rachel Ward, niece of the Earl of Dudley, was panned for her portrayal of Meggie in the TV blockbuster *The Thorn Birds*. But there were compensations—not least when she fell for the man who played her screen husband, then unknown Australian actor **Bryan Brown**. A month after their screen wedding the couple signed up for real in the chapel on her father's 1,800-acre estate in Oxfordshire. She said: 'I always did fall for my leading man, but this time I really went overboard.'

From Woman's World, *March 1985*

Michael Brandon and **Glynis Barber** fell for each other while co-starring in ITV's *Dempsey and Makepeace*—and then tried to keep secret their romance. Eventually they had to admit it publicly when the rest of the

cast knew, while on screen ironically trying to give the impression they hated each other.
From the Sun, *20 September 1985*

Rula Lenska and **Dennis Waterman** met filming an episode of *Minder*. Said Dennis later: 'We couldn't help it. It happened so suddenly and was so total.' His verdict on cupid's sting: 'It was like being hit in the stomach by a ten-ton bag of cement.'
From Weekly News, *2 February 1985*

Paul Young met actress **Stacey Smith** (one of the great on-off romances of the 1980s) on the modern equivalent of the film or stage set—the video shoot. She had been hired to appear in one of his pop videos, and following that it took him three phone calls (the first two merely turned out to be 'a chat') before he plucked up enough courage to ask her out for a date. She then turned up at the restaurant with—a friend. 'It became a romantic dinner for three,' mused Paul.
From the Daily Mail, *28 January 1986;* News of the World, *12 January 1987*

Finally, just in time for Valentine's Day, it was reported that soul queen **Aretha Franklin**, 44, had ditched her 46-year-old businessman boyfriend for a 'toy boy' less than half her age whom she had met shooting a video for her single, *Jimmy Lee*. He was a 21-year-old black male model from Detroit known appropriately as 'The Kid'. One 'insider' was quoted as saying: 'Aretha has always liked younger guys. But this is cradle snatching.'
From the Sun, *4 February 1987*

Totally Predictable Celebrity Meets

AT A DINNER PARTY
Prince Michael met **Princess Michael** to-be at a series of dinner parties. 'He was a charming man I used to invite to dinner parties or when I had extremely eligible European relatives over. I thought "This young man is all alone. I'll produce the right

Bobby Davro
Comedian and impressionist

Favourite chat-up lines
'How was heaven when you left?'
'Do you believe in 90-second sex? Well, have you got a minute?'
'Would you like to come for a drive in my car? I'll show you something different like the soles of my feet in the wing mirror.'
(To girl) 'Do you know the difference between a man's willie and a leg of chicken?' ('No'). 'Well, how would you like to come on a picnic. . . ?'

Best lines tried on me
'How do you get into those trousers?'
—'start by buying me a drink.'
'What makes love like a tiger and winks?'
(Followed, of course, by a wink).

Personal recipe for attracting the opposite sex
Open your wallet to reveal a condom. Smile at them and wink a lot.

girlfriend for him",' she said later. 'I saw myself as a sort of fairy godmother waving my wand.'

From the Daily Mail, *31 July 1984*

AT THE LAUNDERETTE
Don't say it never happens . . . Country singing star **Dolly Parton** met her husband-to-be **Carl Dean** when she was washing her clothes in the laundromat on her first day in Nashville. She stepped out while they washed, and walking down the street, caught the eye of 'a really good-looking guy in a big Chevrolet.' 'He waved at me and I hollered back,' she said later. 'I didn't know you shouldn't speak to strangers in a big city. But it wouldn't have mattered

if I did. I just fell in love with him right away, and he fell in love with me.' They married two years later.

From Weekly News, *7 April 1984*

AT A HOUSE PARTY

John McEnroe met his match, **Tatum O'Neal**, at a house party thrown by Alana Stewart. Tatum sealed the romance by turning up at his apartment with twenty-two pieces of luggage.

From the News of the World, *24 February 1985*

AT DRAMA SCHOOL

Eastenders 'Dirty Den' actor **Leslie Grantham** met his actress wife **Jane Laurie** at drama school—then stood her up three times before they eventually started dating. He said later: 'I'm a very insecure person. I don't have a good opinion of myself, and when an attractive woman talks to me, I think it's a wind-up.'

From the Daily Star, *11 February 1986*

IN A COFFEE BAR

Raquel Welch was a young struggling Hollywood starlet enjoying a cup of coffee in a downtown Espresso bar when in walked the man who was destined to guide her to international stardom, **Patrick Curtis**. He was just the office boy at Rogers and Cowan, but quit to become her Svengali. Others said it was 'business at first sight', but Raquel vouchsafed: 'We did have a very lovely romance.'

From Peter Haining, 'Raquel Welch: Sex Symbol to Superstar', *1984*

Frazer Hines

Actor, star of ITV's 'Emmerdale Farm'
Favourite chat-up lines
'I'll take you out for supper if you make the breakfast.'
'How would you like to be the grandfather of my children?' (This was said by my father to my mother's father when he first saw my mother).

AT A CRICKET MATCH

Well, where else would you expect cricketing super hero **Ian Botham** to meet his future wife? Unsuspectingly **Kathy** had collected her mother from the school where she was teaching and took her to meet her father who was watching the Somerset game. 'We were sitting down when this chap came and plonked himself down. I didn't even know he played,' she said.

From Woman's Own, *1 December 1984*

IN A RESTAURANT

This is where leading authoress-to-be **Frances Edmonds** first clocked her major source of stories, husband-to-be, Test star-to-be, **Phil**. She said: 'With true Rabelaisean fervour he was whacking into a gargantuan deep-pan pizza, and a double portion of chips, the lot awash in a slick of olive oil and tomato ketchup.' What most impressed her, of course, was the double chips. (He'd had his three Shredded Wheat as a starter, obviously.)

From Frances Edmonds, 'Another Bloody Tour',
1986

Clive Warren
Commercial radio DJ

Favourite chat-up line

In a bar in Cyprus, a bloke goes up to a smart girl (tourist) and says: 'Hi, darlin'—I'm in oil.' He was. She later found out that he was a petrol pump attendant down near the quay!

Worst chat-up line

Bloke: 'Do you want to have sex?'
Girl: 'No! Certainly not!'
Bloke: 'Well, would you mind lying down so I can have some?'

Best line tried on me

Once in a really up-market nightclub I was left alone talking to a highly fetching girl and blurted out: 'Do you come here often?' She laughed and laughed in my face as I turned a bright shade of red. Then she brought herself together and said: 'It's all right, you can touch me with your bargepole any time!'

AT THE PUB
Nick Lyndhurst of BBC 1's *Only Fools and Horses*, met his long-term girlfriend **Gail Parr** during a pub crawl in Chichester. She was the first girl for some time *not* to say to him: 'When is your next series on the box?' He was dumbfounded but, alas, didn't pluck up the courage to ask for her phone number. So the lovelorn plonker (no, I didn't mean it, Nick, honest!) went back to the same pub every Sunday night for three months until she appeared again.

From the Sun, *8 September 1984*

ON A SKI SLOPE
Tennis superstar **Chrissie Evert** was one of many, I suspect, to fall in love with their ski instructor. The difference was that this was to lead to his divorce and a big, big romance. She met hunky **Andy Mill** over Christmas 1986 in Colorado and soon he

---

John Francome
Former champion jockey turned stud-owner

Favourite chat-up lines
Boy: 'You're a good-looking girl, do you want to come out for a drink tonight?'
Girl: 'No, get lost.'
Boy: 'Oh, go on, we'll have a really good time.' (Boy goes away and comes back 30 seconds later). 'Excuse me. Has my horrible twin brother been around here pestering you?' (Girl smiles and you're halfway there!).

Boy: 'Would you like a drink, darling?'
Girl: 'Yes, please.'
Boy: 'Well, while you're at the bar get me a whisky and ginger.'

was on the international circuit with her as another love match blossomed.

From the People, *21 June 1987; the* Sun, *6 March 1987*

(Incidentally, **Richard Burton** met and fell for **Suzy Hunt** in a ski-lift.)

ON A LUXURY YACHT

US presidential contender **Gary Hart** fell from grace in 1987 after it was revealed he had been seeing rather a lot of a young actress and model named **Donna Rice**.

'Hi, I know you—you're Senator Gary Hart' was the decisive opening gambit during a party on board a yacht. You know the rest. He asked for her phone number. She gave it to him. He then asked her to make up a party on board a yacht called— wait for it—*Monkey Business*. Someone started taking photos . . .

From the Daily Mail, *5 May 1987; the* Guardian, *6 May 1987*

AT A POLO MATCH

Well, of course. The world's favourite recent romance between **Prince Andrew** and Miss **Sarah Ferguson** did not start because the Princess of Wales pushed her in front of him on the ski slopes, nor because he got absorbed in suggesting, at a pre-Ascot lunch at Windsor Castle, what she should do with her chocolate profiteroles. Her mother, Mrs **Susan Barrantes**, in reply to the question 'Where did they meet?' came out with the immortal words: 'Why at polo, of course. Doesn't everybody?'

From Tim Satchell, 'A Royal Romance', 1986

Totally Unpredictable Celebrity Meets

AT THE BRITISH ROCK AND POP AWARDS

One of the most talked-about romances of 1986, between fifty-year-old guitarist **Bill Wyman** and a young teenager named **Mandy Smith**, had begun, it was later revealed, when he picked her up at this

Chat-up Spot

Q magazine reported in July 1987 that the following had been thrown onstage at **Bruce Springsteen**'s Madison Square Garden concert on 18 December 1980:

1 bedsheet painted with the words 'Merry Christmas, Bruce Springsteen'
5 Santa Claus hats, three of them stencilled 'Bruce'
1 box of 12 Twinkies
1 box of 12 Hostess Cupcakes
3 two-feet long Christmas stockings
1 18" Christmas card, with four rubber gnome musicians taped to it
2 ordinary Christmas cards
1 gift-wrapped package the size and shape of a shoe box
1 stuffed dog
1 rubber duck

annual music biz shindig—thinking she was much older, of course. He invited her to the disco *Tramp* but she said she wasn't feeling well (and it was getting close to her bedtime.) She left her phone number with him, though, and a famous romance was born, not to mention a well-hyped modelling and singing career.

From Sunday Magazine, *14 December 1986*

IN A CAR SHOWROOM
This was the unusual setting for the match between Manchester United's **Jesper Olsen** and blonde model **Sarah Clarke** (well, he was well-known for staying away from discos and clubs). She said: 'Jesper and I hit it off from the very beginning. He was quiet and unassuming, unlike most footballers you meet.' (Most footballers you meet in discos, she means).

From Weekend, *4 February 1987*

ON THE SET OF 'THIS IS YOUR LIFE'
(Irish accent) 'And you weren't expecting to see him tonight . . . he's in Australia, but

we've flown him 5,000 miles . . . (Can you embrace now please) . . .' Yes, on a show honouring **Michael Aspel**, **Eamonn Andrews** found himself in the unfamiliar role of cupid to guests **Lisa Goddard** and **Alvin Stardust**—who later married.

From Weekend, *29 April 1987*

BUYING A HEARSE

Yes, it might seem a little macabre but this is where **Dave Vanian** of the heavy metal group *The Damned* met his American wife **Laurie** in 1977 when they both answered the same used-hearse ad. They took their shared interest seriously enough to actually buy the vehicle jointly, becoming engaged a week after that and marrying only two weeks later.

From No. 1 *magazine, 28 February 1987*

ON THE SCHOOL BUS

Another less colourful version is that they met in a Sussex pub when she asked for his autograph. But this, believe it or not, is hell-raiser **Oliver Reed**'s most recent account of how he came to meet his young love, **Josephine Burge**, then just fifteen: 'I

Richard O'Sullivan
Stage, film and TV actor,
including 'Me and My Girl'

Favourite chat-up line
'I believe that's your house for sale across the road.'
Worst chat-up line
'I believe that's your house for sale across the road.'
Personal recipe for attracting the opposite sex
Indifference!

---

ran out of the pub, jumped on the bus, grabbed her school satchel, shouted: "I'm going to marry you" and jumped off again. The strap of her satchel was tight round her neck at the time.'

And what did the poor girl say?

'All she could say was "aaakkk",' told Ollie, feigning clutching his throat.

From the Daily Mirror, *15 January 1987*

13

The Small Ads

'**Jewish** academic wants to meet woman who's interested in Mozart, James Joyce and sodomy.'

> *Mock ad for Woody Allen in* 'Annie Hall'

'**Divorced** white female, beautiful, statuesque blonde. Witty, cultured. Owns own vibrator.'

> *Mock ad for Kim Basinger in* 'Nine ½ Weeks'

Well, if what now should be your mastery of the spoken sublime isn't getting you anywhere, why not advertise? The Lonely Hearts market is now such an industry that one British magazine, *Time Out*, logs 10,000 small ads (and that's 200,000 replies) every year.

Remember, it was through an ad that Lucy Irvine (of *Castaway* fame) found the path to riches and glory: 'Writer seeks "wife" for year on tropical island' landed her one of the decade's great adventures. Why not you?

Though if you really want to see some inventive copywriting, look to the 'county' press. Here is really getting to grips with the priorities in life. Like this example from the Royal Society for the Protection of Birds magazine in September 1976:

'**Border cross duck** (Derbyshire/Yorkshire) would like Drake (40–55). Interests include ornithology, travel, yoga.' Or
'**Frisky heifer** (well, young 41-year-old) seeks Red Star Bull to share her pastures in West Country, either just social or merger/partnership if compatibull.'

> *From* Country Landowner, *January 1987*

Chat-up Facts

There was a fascinating survey in *Woman's World* in March, 1985, when **Maggie Alderson** and **Ruby Millington** boogied their way across the country to investigate the 'hot spots' for men's 'pick-up prowess'.

London machos emerged the most forward, descending on the heroic twosome within 30 seconds of their entering the door. In Newcastle it took the men 1 minute 12 seconds to try to score, in Cardiff 2 mins 40 seconds, in Portsmouth 17 mins 9 seconds, while in unhip Birmingham the girls reported:

'After two hours and four minutes nothing had happened.' The best Brummie chat-up line in the whole of the night was a pathetic 'Can I have a light?' 'When they asked us the time, it was because they didn't want to miss the last bus home,' lamented the two investigators. DJ Tony Blackburn agreed with the assessment, telling the *Daily Mail*: 'The only thing you can ask a Birmingham girl is whether she has a cold. Another good chat-up line is to discuss ways of getting out of Birmingham. Very few people manage it.'

That is not to beat perhaps the cleverest rural LH ad, spotted in the *Mountain Echo* of Himeville in the Drakensberg Mountains of South Africa, and reprinted in the *Daily Telegraph*. It read:

'**Man** of 38 wishes to meet woman of 30 owning tractor. Please enclose photograph of tractor.'

Bizarrest Lonely Hearts Ads

Man needs woman.
From Time Out, *28 May 1985*

Hywell seeks Blodwen for Welsh duet.
From Time Out, *7 November 1984*

Felicity Kendal-type covets Melvyn Bragg type.
From Time Out, *25 November 1987*

The 34th most tedious man in London, 29, seeks boring female for mind-boringly strained conversations on palimpsests, pursuivants and Paternoster Square.
From Time Out, *23 March 1988*

Bachelor, young 60, sabretoothed Thatcherite bordering neo-fascist, seeks uncaring female 40+ for dwarf throwing, seal clubbing and other insensitive, uncompassionate activities.
From Private Eye, *quoted by Peterborough,* Daily Telegraph

Young man, looks like James Dean, talks like James Dean, dresses like James Dean, seeks girl for very short motoring holiday.
LH ad quoted by Chris Tarrant, Capital Radio

Sagittarian, 46, divorced, fleeced, limp (walks with), failing eyesight, been doctored, shares Quasimodo's tailor, bitter, temporary mysognist, recently mugged, answers to name Lucky.
From Singles, *quoted in the* Daily Telegraph

Disabled alcoholic (40), occasionally violent when drunk, seeks physical relationship with big-busted nymphomaniac who runs pub. Please send photo of pub.

From Private Eye, *1 May 1987*

A Somewhat Kinky Touch

Attractive adventurous romantic male, late 40s, tall, slim, active, virile, seeks slim non-smoking attractive sensual and affectionate female, 25–38, with sense of humour for magic moments. Suspenders definite asset. London/South East.

From Private Eye, *13 June 1986*

Submissive male, slim, seeks understanding schoolmistress to administer needs.

From City Limits, *24 May 1985*

Male, slim, 38, friendly, spankable, would like to meet female with kissable bottom. Looks and age not important.

From City Limits, *10 May 1985*

Transvestite, young, attractive, slim, seeks female to help with dressing up, make-up etc.

From Time Out, *8 November 1984*

Bisexual female, 28, blonde, attractive, university graduate, own house with unlimited booze, seeks DOMINANT tough girlfriend/mistress. BIKERS/ LEATHERWOMEN welcome.

From City Limits, *10 May 1985*

Toyboy, 25, single, Scorpio, SW1, seeks stern female influence, short hair and/or foreign preferred.

From Private Eye, *13 June 1986*

Jewish guy, 32, warm, sensitive, intelligent, interests politics, psychotherapy, wants to meet attractive, interesting woman who can't take NOT being slippered.

From City Limits, *10 May 1985*

Mister Leather, 28, own dungeon equipment and harnesses, seeks well-hung torturers. Drag queens welcome. Strictly no freaks.

From Gay *magazine quoted in the* Sunday Mirror, *October 1982*

Geddit! 'Strictly no freaks'

Chat-up Line

One man with just about the most novel approach was revealed by Scotland Yard in June 1986. He was a motorcyclist who targeted young women, pretended to have broken down, and then asked them *to sit on his head.* Many apparently did so.

A typical incident was recounted: the man (description: 'defective left eye and wearing a metallic blue crash helmet') claimed his bike had broken down and asked the girl to sit on the back. 'He then asked her to sit on his shoulder, which she did,' said a police spokesman, 'and then asked her to sit on his head.

'At this the woman thought there was something amiss and ran off.'

Others were apparently more gullible. Said the police: 'He must have a very good line in chat because he cons his victims into doing quite a few bizarre things before they twig.'

From the Barnet Times, *22 June 1987*

14

Unhappy Endings

Not all romantic introductions end happily, of course. All modern sophisticates are advised to consider some salutary lessons.

'This is the girl for you, Cecil.' It was those fateful words in 1971 from **John Marling**, head of the Government Whips Office at Westminster, about a pretty young secretary called **Sara Keays**, which were eventually to rebound in a Cabinet Minister's temporary disgrace and a whiff of public scandal.

Still on the subject of politics, a gentleman 'who had taken grandly of wine' at a reception at Holyrood House told **Mrs Thatcher**, in no uncertain terms, that he fancied her and would like to go to bed with her. The Prime Minister was cool in a crisis as always. 'Quite right,' she said. 'You have

very good taste—but I just do not think you would make it at the moment.'

One of the most spectacular Royal romancing rebuffs came on the Royal Yacht *Britannia* when the roving eye of the then happy bachelor **Prince Andrew** caught sight of a curvy brunette Palace maid, according to the ship's biographer, Andrew Morton. Later in the day he took his valet aside and asked him: 'Do you think you could arrange for that young lady to bring me breakfast in bed in the morning?' Unfortunately she refused, and later told colleagues ' . . . I wasn't interested. I've already got a boyfriend.'

One of the saddest celebrity stories I have heard concerned one pianist/crooner **Gilbert O'Sullivan** and a girl called **Sue**, whom he used to see every day on the tube. He told interviewer **Ray Connolly** in the London *Evening Standard* that each day he got on at Notting Hill Gate, and she got off at Kensington High Street, and he spent six months plucking up courage to say hello. Then one day she didn't get off, and as the train sped on past Gloucester Road and South Ken, he started chatting to her.

'A bit later on I took her for a coffee and said I'd take her out to the pictures but for some reason I never did. And she was just the girl for me, perfect.' Later little Gilbert became rich and famous and a little more confident as a result. One day he came across the girl's photo. Frantically he found out the address of the girl of his dreams and wrote apologizing for not taking more notice of her earlier . . . She wrote back saying she was married.

Bob Geldof tells in his autobiography *Is That It?* how, on his first night out with **Paula Yates**, she was approached in a night club by a 'shifty and embarrassed young man' who said: 'Hi, I'm Bono. I'm the singer in a band called U2.' 'So what?' Miss Yates altogether crushingly replied.

Rock-crazy **Chrissie Hynde** of *The Pretenders* had a habit of meeting famous rock stars—with many an unhappy ending. There was the celebrated occasion she and a 16-year-old girlfriend ended up in a hotel room with **Rod Stewart** and **Ron Wood** after a concert. She insisted on leaving 'because I have a driving lesson in the morning'.

She was later to propose to both **Johnny Rotten** and **Sid Vicious**. At the time, they both agreed. Then things became more difficult when poor Sid remembered a previous engagement. She said: 'I could have been Mrs Vicious—if he hadn't had to go to court that day.'

From No. 1 *magazine, 31 January 1987;* Sunday Express *magazine, 16 November 1986*

Girl pop heart-throb **Kim Wilde** had the first proposal of marriage from a young gentleman called **John** in the middle of the Arizona desert. She had met him 'at a gig in Lisle', 'and he was so cute and handsome and there he was in the middle of the desert giving me my first ever proposal of marriage'. She said she thought about it but there was one thing against him: 'He didn't look like **Prince**,' she said. 'I couldn't trust a man who doesn't look like Prince.'

From Today, *30 April 1987*

I find rather sweet the story of **Jimi Hendrix** who at a London club one night plonked himself down between **Mick Jagger** and then girlfriend **Marianne Faithfull**. Turning to Marianne he came up with this immortal line: 'I want to **** you. You should leave him, he's a ****, and come with me right now.' Convent-educated Marianne refused, slightly more demurely I should imagine.

Then there was the time shy crooner **Gilbert O'Sullivan** was propositioned by the self-styled 'happy hooker' **Xaviera Hollander**. She told him: 'Come to bed!' 'But I'm not tired,' he replied.

All-girl group *Bananarama* told the *Sun* in December 1984 of their best chat-up squelches.

Squelch No. 1 came, according to **Keren Woodward**, when 'an awful boring old man' came down and sat next to them at a London night spot. 'He was a ghastly loud American, but I was too polite to tell him to buzz off. I got the shock of my life when his chauffeur approached me later and said Mr **John Denver**, the famous singer, would like to know if I could join him in his Rolls to go to the club.'

Squelch No. 2 came when 'two hair men' burst into their hotel bedroom wearing nothing but scanty briefs. 'They were horrible medallion men,' said **Siobhan Fahey**. 'No brains—but lots of hairy chest and clanking jewellery.'

The trio felt frightened at first, their body-guards having gone off duty. But then they came up with the ideal solution—they burst into a fit of hysterical giggling. Said Keren: 'When men come on strong now we just laugh. That normally insults their male ego and they feel put off.'

Humorist **Colin Reid** told in *Revue* magazine, in February 1984, of this bizarre and doomed chat-up routine used in a bar at

Puerto Banus, Marbella, by a fast-working Spaniard on a young English girl:

'Darling' he said. 'You're the only one for me. I love you, I need you. I can't live without you.'

'Please,' she gasped, pushing the ardent young fellow away.

'What's wrong?' he said.

'I don't want to get serious,' she said.

'Who's serious?' he said.

Finally, a young girl rang snooker star **Tony Knowles** with an unusual plea in chat-up lines. She said she had bet her friend £20 that she could get a night out with him. Tony passed the problem on to an associate. 'If she rings back, tell her she's lost her money,' he growled.

Five Crushingly Romantic Lines from the Film 'Brief Encounter'

1 'Please let me look. I happen to be a doctor.
2 You must eat one of these—fresh this morning.
3 There must be a part of you, deep down inside—some little spirit that still wants to climb out of the window—that still longs to splash about a bit in the dangerous sea.
4 Please, I ask you most humbly.
5 It's no use running away from the truth, darling, we're lovers, aren't we? If it happens or if it doesn't, we're lovers in our hearts.'

Trevor Howard to Celia Johnson (Words by Noel Coward from the play 'Still Life')